SHEFFIELD PUBS

IAN D. ROTHERHAM, CHRISTINE HANDLEY,
& MICHAEL LIVERSIDGE

AMBERLEY

First published 2016

Amberley Publishing
The Hill, Stroud
Gloucestershire, GL5 4EP

www.amberley-books.com

ISBN 978 1 4456 5379 2 (print)
ISBN 978 1 4456 5380 8 (ebook)

British Library Cataloguing in Publication Data.
A catalogue record for this book is available from the British Library.

Origination by Amberley Publishing.
Printed in the UK.

Contents

	Map and Key	4
	Introduction	6
Chapter One	The City Centre	9
Chapter Two	From Grenoside and North-East Sheffield to the Lower Don Valley, Attercliffe and Darnall	30
Chapter Three	Woodhouse to Gleadless Townend	42
Chapter Four	Norton to Nether Edge, Ecclesall, Totley and Beyond	49
Chapter Five	From Crookes and the Rivelin Valley Across Northern Sheffield	77
	Bibliography	94
	About the Authors	95

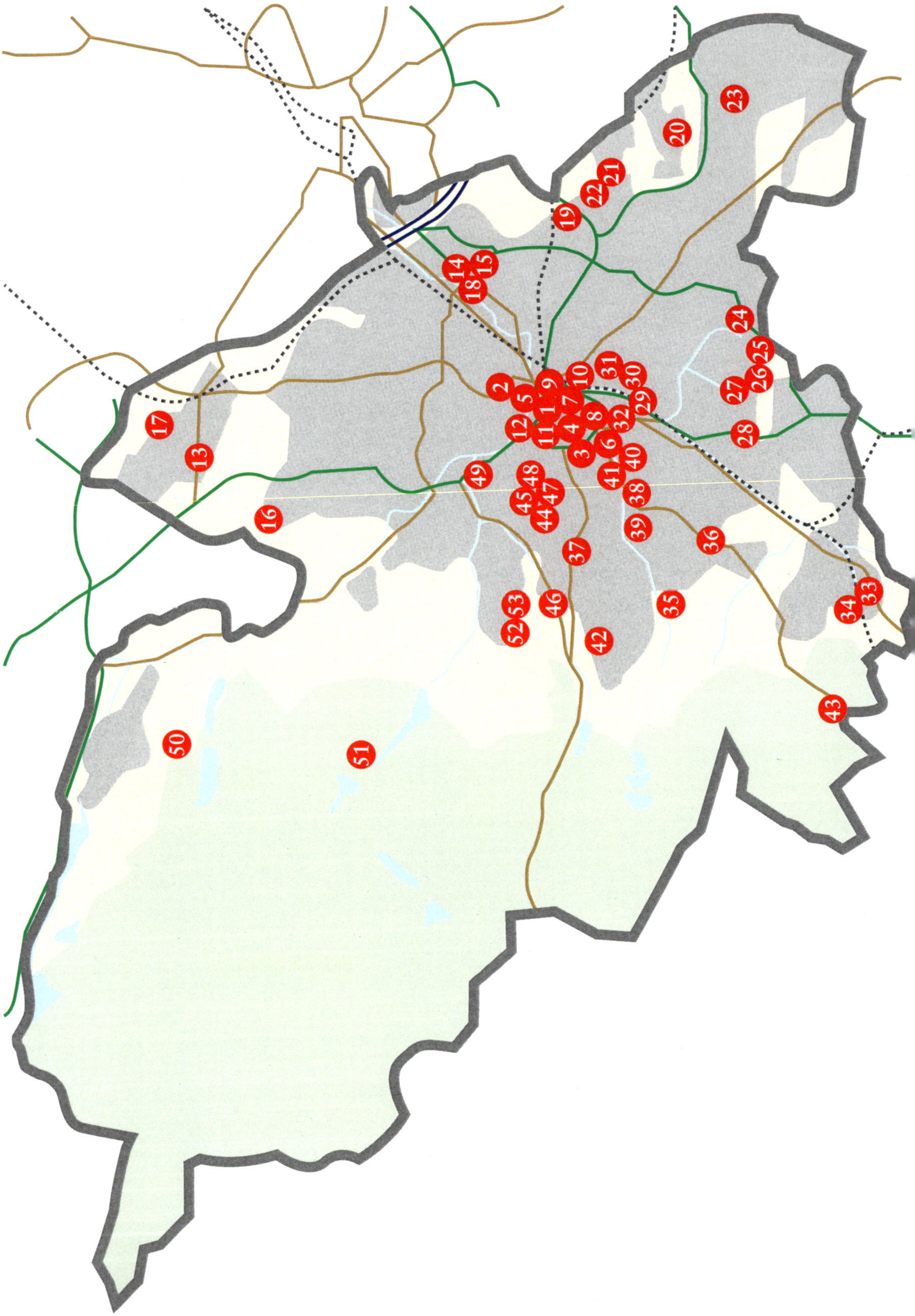
1
2
3
4
5
6
7
8
9
10
11
12
13
14
15
16
17
18
19
20
21
22
23
24
25
26
27
28
29
30
31
32
33
34
35
36
37
38
39
40
41
42
43
44
45
46
47
48
49
50
51
52
53

Chapter One: The City Centre

1. The Church House, St James Street
2. The Fat Cat, Alma Street
3. The Great Gatsby (or Foresters), Division Street
4. Sheffield Waterworks Company, Division Street
5. The Museum, Orchard Square / Street
6. The Nursery Tavern, Ecclesall Road
7. The Old Queen's Head, Pond Hill
8. The Red Lion, Charles Street
9. The Royal Victoria Hotel, Victoria Station Road
10. Sheffield Tap, Sheffield Midland Railway Station
11. The Three Tuns, Silver Street Head
12. The Ship Inn, Shalesmoor

Chapter Two: From Grenoside and north-east Sheffield to the Lower Don Valley, Attercliffe and Darnall

13. The Acorn, Bracken Hill, Burncross
14. Arena Square, Attercliffe Common
15. Carbrook Hall, Carbrook Road , Attercliffe
16. The Old Harrow, Main Street, Grenoside
17. The Packhorse, Packhorse Lane, High Green
18. The Wentworth House Hotel, Milford Street
19. The White Rose, Handsworth Road, Darnall

Chapter Three: Woodhouse to Gleadless Townend

20. The Angel, Woodhouse
21. The Cross Keys, Handsworth
22. The Sword Dancer, Handsworth
23. The Gypsy Queen, Beighton
24. The Red Lion, Gleadless Townend

Chapter Four: Norton to Nether Edge, Ecclesall, Totley and beyond

25. The Bagshawe Arms, Norton Lane
26. The Nailmakers, Backmoor, Hemsworth
27. The Sportsman, Harvey Clough Road, Norton Lees
28. The Big Tree, Chesterfield Road, Woodseats
29. The White Lion, Chesterfield Road, Heeley
30. The Shakespeare or Brothers, Well Road, Heeley
31. The Sheaf View, Gleadless Road, Heeley
32. The Broadfield, Abbeydale Road, Highfield
33. The Cross Scythes, Baslow Road, Totley
34. The Cricket Inn, Penny Lane, Totley
35. The Norfolk Arms, Ringinglow
36. The Rising Sun, Abbey Lane, Parkhead
37. The Hammer & Pincers, Ringinglow Road, Bents Green
38. The Banner Cross Hotel, Ecclesall Road
39. The Greystones, Greystones Road
40. The Stag's Head Inn, Psalter Lane
41. The Pointing Dog Clubhouse, Ecclesall Road
42. The Shiny Sheff, Crimicar Lane, Lodge Moor
43. The Fox House Inn, Hathersage Road, Longshaw

Chapter Five: From Crookes and the Rivelin Valley across northern Sheffield

44. The Ball Inn, Crookes
45. The Cobden View, Cobden View Road, Crookes
46. The Rivelin, Tofts Lane, Stannington
47. The Closed Shop, Commonside, Walkley
48. The Hallamshire House, Commonside, Walkley
49. The Rawsons Spring, Langsett Road, Hillsborough
50. The Castle, Stone Moor Road, Bolsterstone
51. The Old Horns, High Bradfield
52. The Crown & Glove, Uppergate Road, Stannington
53. The Peacock, Stannington Road, Stannington

Introduction

A Brief History of Sheffield

Sheffield is in the north of the English Midlands and is located on the confluence of a number of major and lesser rivers. Urban development was restricted to small riverside settlements of a few thousand people in the local townships in and around Sheffield, with some settlements possibly originating in Roman times around 1500 years ago. There has been a long-term transformation of the region and its main city, Sheffield, with outlying districts being amalgamated into the city and county boundary changes expanding the city borders hugely. We have included public houses that are within the present-day boundary of the city. Through industrialisation and urbanisation, over a period of around 500 years, Sheffield grew from being primarily rural to massively industrial, and then to post-industrial in the late twentieth century. Recent changes have included post-industrial urban renewal with the catalysts of sport, leisure, tourism, education and environment. These have combined to transform both places and people. Sheffield and its region was a steel manufacturing powerhouse for England, for the Empire and for the world beyond. As the British Empire spread around the planet, materials manufactured and produced here spread as a global brand. The city today, once noted for its appalling pollution, is one of the greenest industrial cities in Europe. This history is reflected in the public houses and drinking habits across the region.

The Pubs and Inns of Sheffield

With its long history and heritage, Sheffield has a rich diversity of public houses, hotels and other hostelries. Indeed, choosing around fifty premises has been a difficult process of selection. Many excellent pubs are omitted, including many favourites of the authors', but to cover more would render the volume unwieldy. Additionally, we have tried to cover a spread of the geographic coverage of Sheffield – which is a very big city and a huge area – and a range of types, styles and histories. So if your favourite pub is omitted, then maybe look out for volume two!

Sheffield's long history from a rural area with small, family-run and specialist industrial sites to a growing town with industry and commerce, and the twentieth-century industrialisation and urbanisation, has left a distinctive legacy of associated public houses. Alongside the commercial and industrial growth has been the emergence of education; Sheffield has two major universities that cater to over 50,000 students. The demand for nightlife and the recent trend for urban city centre living have triggered a renaissance in urban hostelries, which has also influenced our choice of examples. Many old pubs have gone, some being casualties of urban redevelopments, and others lost to changing tastes for leisure and recreation. At the same time, new pubs have appeared, associated with modern housing estates or new commercial developments, a constant ebb and flow of venues and hostelries. A one-time resident and visitor to Sheffield today might find their favourite pub unchanged, 'modernised', 'revamped', or gone completely. In other cases, entirely new premises will have appeared. Sadly the old names change and, while this has always been an on-going process of acquisition and naming, in many cases the old names and even the pub signs are remarkable connections to a cultural past that is too easily forgotten. Replacing names such as the 'Carpenters' Arms' with the 'Slug and Sprocket' maybe loses the point.

Some Drinking Traditions of the City

In recent years, many public houses have found it hard to survive changing demographics, cheap supermarket beers, and especially increased stay-at-home entertainment. However, there are signs of some recovery and while many continue to close (in some cases be demolished), we hope many pubs will survive. A major influence on past drinking habits and on the legacy of public houses was the effect of mass heavy industry in parts of the Sheaf Valley, the Upper Don Valley and especially the Lower Don Valley. Combined with the tendency for large numbers of workers to reside close to the places of employment, this situation led to 'a pub on every corner'. Workers poured out of factories, often having worked on physically demanding jobs in desperately hot conditions, and headed to the local to put away a few pints of locally brewed best bitter. Legislation in 1830, which allowed people to open 'beerhouses' for selling beer but not spirits, also contributed to the increase in the number of small pubs. These were often opened in the front rooms of existing cottages and houses as a way of supplementing income for families who also worked in a trade.

Several of the pubs in this book started life this way. There were also major local and distinctive breweries, with several surviving and even thriving up until the latter part of the twentieth century: Wards, Stones, Tennant Brothers, Tetleys and Whitbreads to mention just a few. Their ultimate loss to the greed of the big corporations is something not easily forgotten or forgiven. However, in the period from the turn of the millennium to today, there has been a resurgence in local brewing originally pioneered by the people at the Fat Cat and Kelham Island. There was, of course, the Frog and Parrot on Division Street, with 'Roger and out' brewed on the premises. The big players have one-by-one disappeared and replaced by a new generation of local high-quality brewers from micros to craft breweries. A couple of the pubs have names that reflect the older tradition, now revived, of brewing beer on-site so the beer was 'on tap'. These pubs, known as brewery taps, showcased the range of products available from the brewery. We have tried to provide a wide selection of these new beers and their outlets in our choice of pubs.

The post-work rush of thirsty workers to the corner pubs has now been replaced by hordes of students after lectures, but the typical local is thriving too. While many old pubs have gone, and the continuing loss is a tragedy for local communities and especially the distinctiveness of local heritage and sense of place, there seems to be some recovery. Quite a few 'locals' have worked hard to rediscover their particular identity and their place as a centre for local people and communities. This is something that is especially important in the suburbs and more peripheral rural areas. Also, in many cases, pubs have diversified to offer food alongside drinks – a radical change from the days of pork scratchings, pickled eggs, the Friday night cockle seller, crisps and peanuts! Having emerged from the days when 'chicken in a basket' was considered the latest sophisticated affectation, our public houses now offer food from good-quality basic stuff, to high-end restaurant fare.

There have been many books on Sheffield's history and several on pubs and drinking in the city. We are grateful to the authors of all of these, and hope this volume will add to the lineage and encourage further interest.

Chapter One

The City Centre

The Church House, St James Street

This is a relatively new public house opened in a characterful, Grade II-listed building close to Sheffield Cathedral. In 1983, the premises were a squat for the Sheffield Anarchists, when they established an Anarchist Centre here. The Church House, as it is now known, started life as a licensed premises in the early 1990s, when this old Grade II-listed church building was converted into a very nice, comfortable, public house

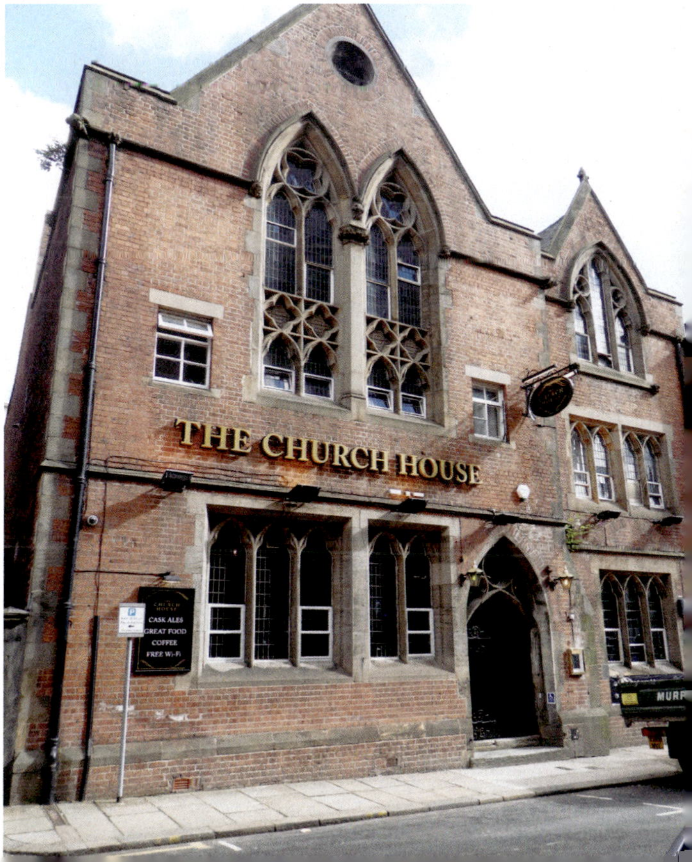

The Church House viewed from St James Street.

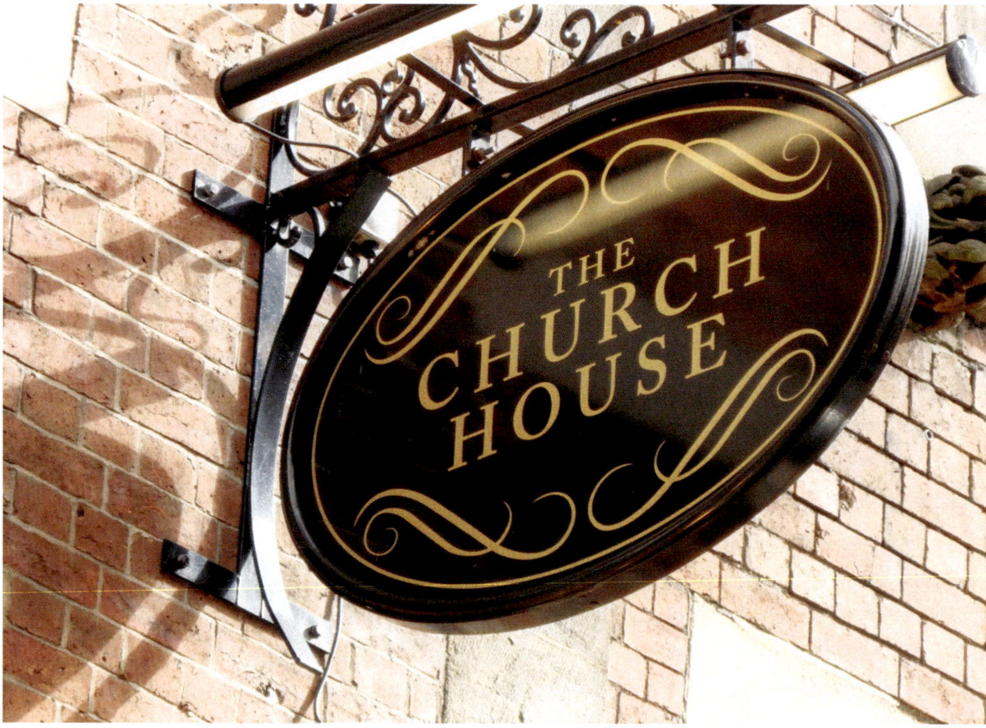

The Church House inn sign.

called the Gladstones. There is no evidence that it was referring to the prime minister, William Gladstone, as there is also the Gladstone Building opposite the Church House. It has had four further names and incarnations as a public house since then: the Ferret and Trouserleg, The Priory, The Sanctuary, and currently The Church House.

The Church House has been totally renovated and has a lovely interior, which offers its drinkers and diners a beautiful venue to relax in. The clientele ranges from office workers, during dinnertime and early evenings, to the younger drinkers who arrive to listen to the live music that the Church House offers on a regular basis. Although some of the reviews so far have been a little mixed, the setting clearly has plenty of atmosphere with the usual beers, wines and spirits plus unpretentious food.

The Fat Cat, Alma Street

Formerly the Alma, the renamed Fat Cat was the brainchild of university economics lecturer David Wickett and his business collaborator, Bruce Bentley, a Sheffield solicitor. The acquisition of the Alma and the development of The Fat Cat and then the Kelham Island Brewery was a key moment in the recovery of real ale in Sheffield pubs and the tradition of small, local breweries. The premises were previously a part of the William Stones Cannon Brewery, a lineage extending back to around 1875. Wickett and Bentley purchased the Alma in the early 1980s, paying only £33,750 for a property that was then in a decidedly run-down, post-industrial area. However, the move was certainly

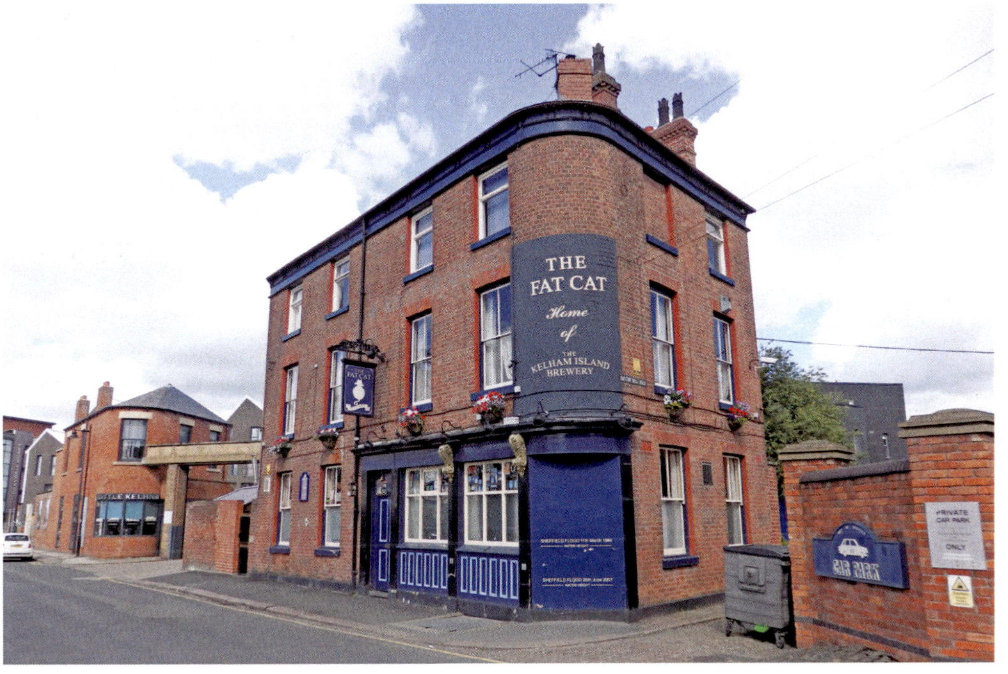

Above: The Fat Cat on Alma Street.

Below: The Fat Cat inn sign.

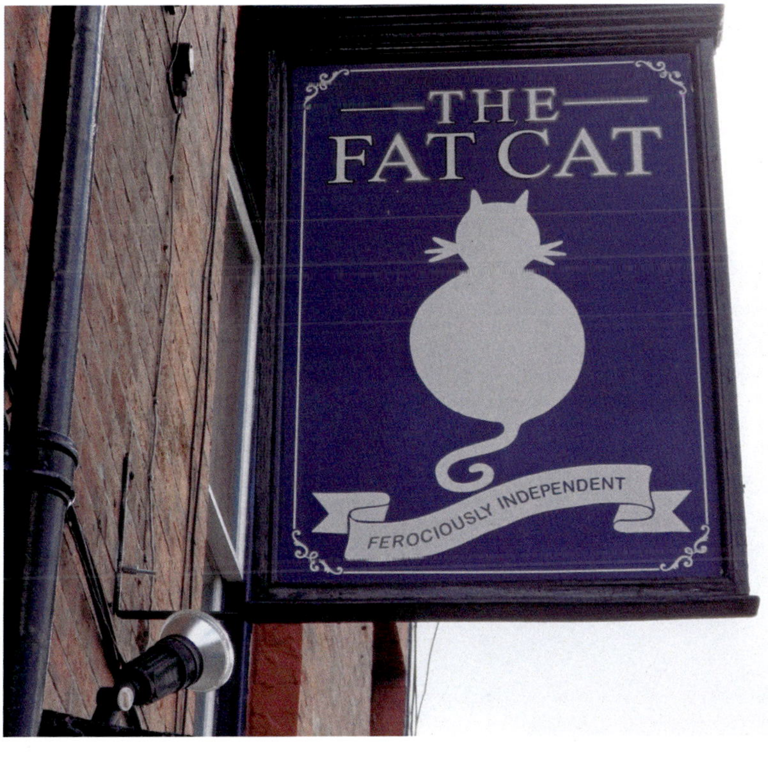

visionary with the River Don location now in the heart of Sheffield's post-industrial renaissance. The new pub had an emphasis of good real ales and food at a reasonable price; it remains hugely popular.

This particular public house has come a long way since it opened as The Fat Cat on 21 August 1981. The duo were trying to provide an alternative to the pubs owned by the big breweries, which at the time dominated Sheffield. Beers were introduced that were new to the area, including those from small independent breweries, and a guest beer policy was introduced. This was a first in Sheffield, and allowed a wide range of choice. The Fat Cat became the first outlet in Sheffield for beers such as Fullers, Boddingtons, Greene King, Marstons, Theakstons and Timothy Taylors. Traditional scrumpy cider and unusual bottled beers were also introduced. After Dave Wickett bought out Bruce Bentley in December 1989, the pub introduced a 'no smoking room', the first in the area. Open fires were also reintroduced for winter and it was decided to have no music, fruit machines or other electronic games. The key event happened when, in 1990, a brewery was built in what had been the beer garden and the first brew was produced in September of that year.

The Fat Cat is now known nationally for its quality real ales, traditional pub atmosphere and its setting, in the heart of Kelham Island, which had begun to develop as an industrial manufacturing area in the eighteenth century. And today, the Kelham Island Industrial Museum is close by. One of the initial beers produced was the horribly named First Worts. This name refers to the beer before yeast is added. This award-winning Sheffield pub has a great mixture of young and old patrons, free parking, amazing beer and great food.

The brewery still produces a range of specialist beers with a growing reputation for quality, often featuring in publications and also winning several awards, including the CAMRA Champion Beer of Britain (GOLD – Supreme Champion) for Pale Rider. Along with the original Fat Cat and the new brewery, located on Alma Street, there is now a shop and function room, which is available for party bookings.

On The Fat Cat's website it states 'the building currently known as The Fat Cat was completed in the year 1850 and began life as a public house known as 'The Alma', possibly because it is located on Alma Street. The Alma later became a hotel.' These details are fine but we think the street was not named Alma until after the battle that took place during the Crimean War. This would make the name slightly later as the Battle of the Alma, usually considered the first battle of the Crimean War, didn't take place until 20 September 1854. Presumably the street and the public house were renamed retrospectively. Therefore the historic information is just a few years out. It was owned by local industrialists and rooms at the pub were used as lodgings for local workers from the late 1850s to the early twentieth century.

The Great Gatsby (or Foresters), Division Street

The Great Gatsby is situated on the corner of Division Street and Rockingham Street and has been through the usual pub name changes that now seem to be normal. Originally the Foresters Inn or Arms, it has also been the Yorick, Olive and Hush Bar, and now The Great Gatsby. Today's name 'The Great Gatsby' was the title of a famous 1925 novel written by American author F. Scott Fitzgerald. However, the pub's original name may have been derived from the 'Ancient Order of Foresters', a self-help philanthropic organisation, rather than any direct connection with the occupation of forester.

Situated right in the heart of Sheffield The Great Gatsby is a bar to suit all tastes; it is a night-time snug with a vast liquor range, and a weekend party bar with the best music and a 3 a.m. licence. The kitchen has become the home of Shy Boy Cantina – street food experts serving the best in Mexican-inspired dishes. The Gatsby also boasts a very nice beer garden. Mostly though, it is just a great place to hang out in the Sheffield city centre, so pop in and say hello! One of the authors of this book remembers that, in the 1960s, the pub was so sparse, seating-wise, it seemed to have only old railway carriage seating on a few of the walls. This was not a comfortable pub at all, but one that was strangely a well frequented pub.

This pub is dated back to at least 1828. When builders were excavating for a new extension in the early 1980s, the landlord was surprised (*The Star* said 'shell-shocked'), by the discovery of abundant oyster shells in the material dug out. Apparently the building was situated next to a shellfish dealer in the early 1900s and the oyster shells were probably dumped at that time. In the Victorian period, oysters were one of the most sought after delicacies and some people spent a small fortune on them, and of course drink as well. The present buildings received a major refurbishment in the early 1990s, that part of West Street and Devonshire Green finding a new fashionability and a resurgent nightlife.

Sheffield Water Works Company, Division Street

Previously known as Lloyds No. 1 Café Bar, the name changed to the Sheffield Water Works Company in 2007. This is a big city centre venue; it is close to the leisure facilities, such as the City Hall, and a part of the West Street and Devonshire Green complex of shops, restaurants, clubs and pubs. Today it is a Wetherspoon's pub and is therefore geared towards the provision of cheap and cheerful food and a good selection of beers at low cost; the chain tending towards big, bold, brash and cheap food but good value if a little indifferent. It is set in the remarkable building of the former Sheffield Water Works Company, which must make it one of the most striking of the city's public houses. The company was formed in 1830 and the building dates from then. The premises were taken over by Sheffield Corporation's Transport Department and later became a part of the one-time NUM headquarters. This was, for a few years, Arthur Scargill's headquarters when he led the National Union of Mineworkers. The Sheffield Water Works, part of the City of Sheffield's Corporation (the local authority), offices moved into the Castle Market Building when that opened. Sheffield Water Works 'disappeared' in the 1970s with local government reorganisation and the creation of Yorkshire Water, who remained at the Castle Market building for many years after.

This Old Sheffield Water Works building probably holds as much of Sheffield's history as any other premises in the city. The premises were owned by Mr J. G. Graves, later Alderman, a man who presented the city with more gifts and contributions than probably any other benefactor. These gifts included the Graves Art Gallery and money to buy very large pieces of land such as Graves Park and Blackamoor, which

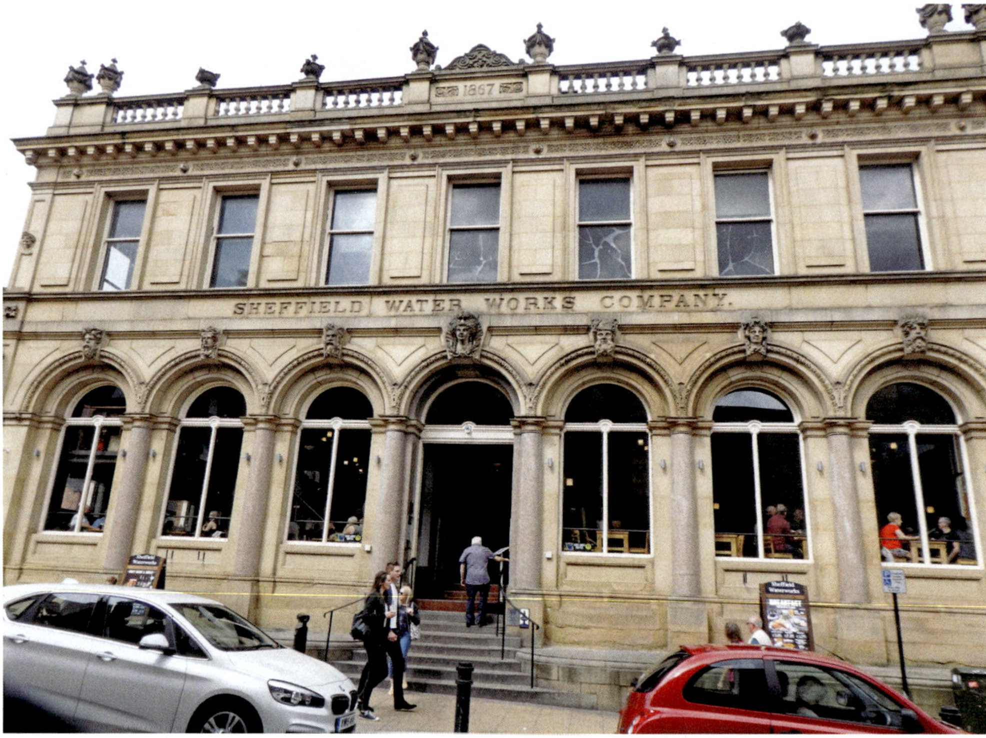

Above: The imposing building that houses the Water Works public house.

Below: Sheffield Water Works' busy bar area.

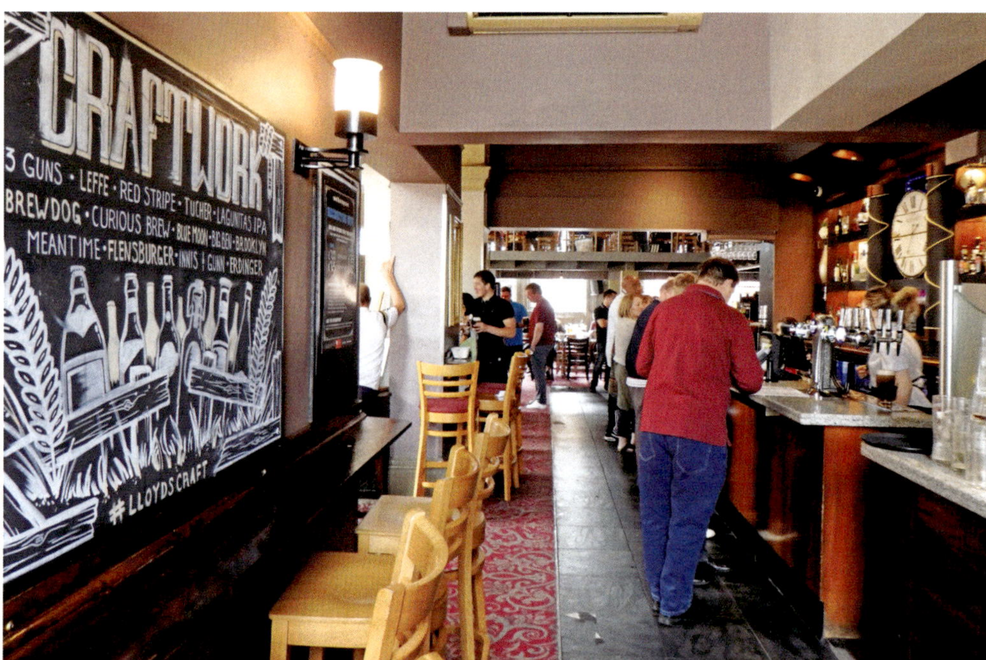

were then on the outskirts of Sheffield. He was one of the city's visionaries and great philanthropists. The J. G. Graves Charitable Trust is still active today. Graves began his postal watch-selling business in this building, a forerunner of all the catalogue businesses throughout England today. A man who took business risks, he would make money but soon lost much of it again. However, he persevered and quickly made his fortune once more. After Graves' retirement, the premises were sold on to more catalogue traders, who in turn sold it on to the Sheffield Water Works Company.

The Wetherspoon company bought this imposing Victorian building, rescuing it from further decline, and it is just what you expect from a business that values its drinkers and its diners: decent, affordable, well-prepared food and a very large range of beers, lagers and ciders. We recommend the upstairs dining area in the evening, offering nice views of the illuminated City Hall, Barker's Pool, and well-lit fountains. All-in-all, this is a pleasant pub in a nice area of Sheffield.

The Museum, Orchard Square / Street

This is a pleasant city centre pub that offers good beers and a wide range of nice food at decent prices. It is in the heart of the 1980s Orchard Square development, which combined the careful conservation of some Sheffield heritage under threat with modern retail and leisure development. When Orchard Square was opened in 2005, the pub was named the Hogshead but has since reverted to the older name 'The

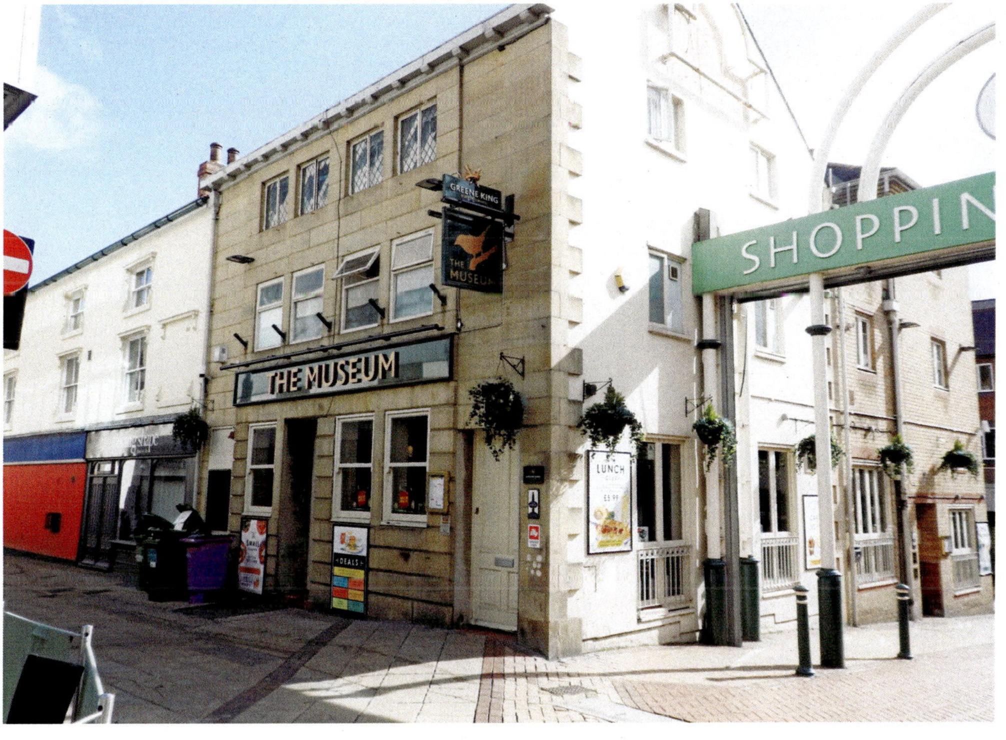

The Museum, Orchard Lane.

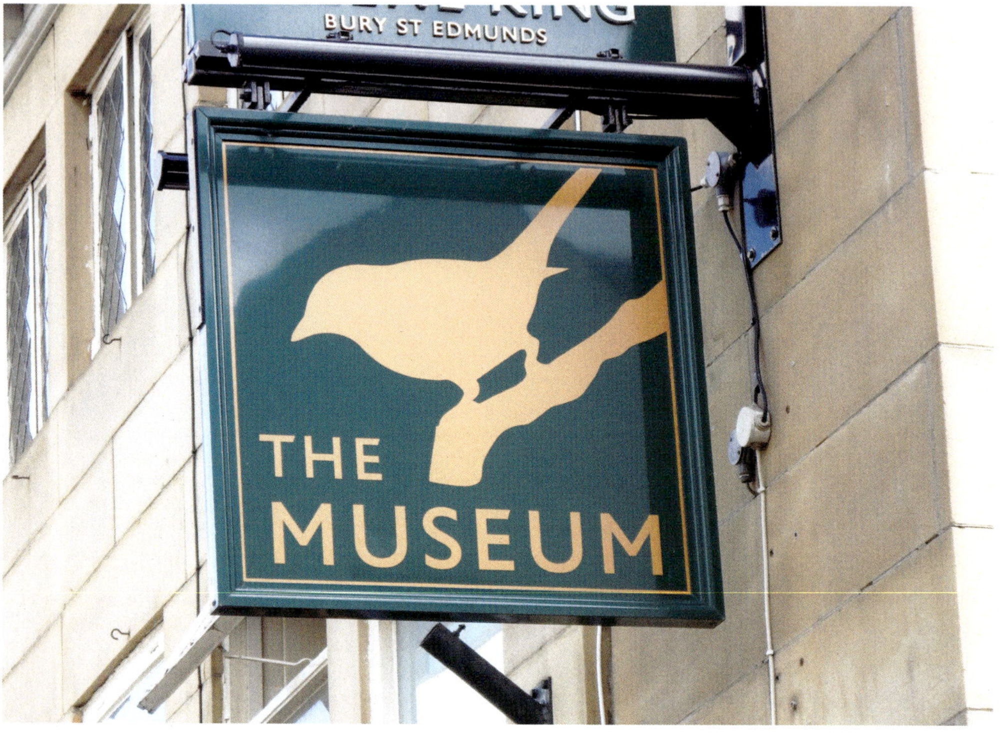

The Museum, Orchard Lane inn sign.

Museum', whose frontage was on Orchard Street in one of the historic parts of the old Sheffield town and, as its name suggests, an area of fruit orchards before the town expanded. The area was saved largely through public pressure rather than (initially at least) enlightened planning. The present-day Museum pub is one of the benefits from that process and the award-winning Orchard Square development. The drinks on offer here include a wide variety of draught and bottled beers, ciders, wines, spirits, and real or craft ales. The Museum is part of the Greene King brewery chain, but provides real ales from the local Kelham Island, Bradfield, and Abbeydale breweries. An interesting thought while you eat and drink is that The Museum was built on the site of the first Sheffield Hospitals' mortuary. The vaulted ceilings in the beer cellar today are the remaining evidence of that former building.

The Nursery Tavern, Ecclesall Road

The Nursery Tavern is a relatively small, three-roomed local pub with a beer garden. It was first opened in 1865 and is full of history, situated close to Sheffield Botanical Gardens and the historic General Cemetery (now a public open space). By the 1950s and 1960s, the Nursery was a popular haunt for local folk after work or at weekends. On Sundays all the men wore suits; Saturday nights were for the ladies with everyone singing along to the piano. Remember, this was pretty much before the widespread ownership of televisions. In the 1970s, the Nursery Tavern was known for its shelves of

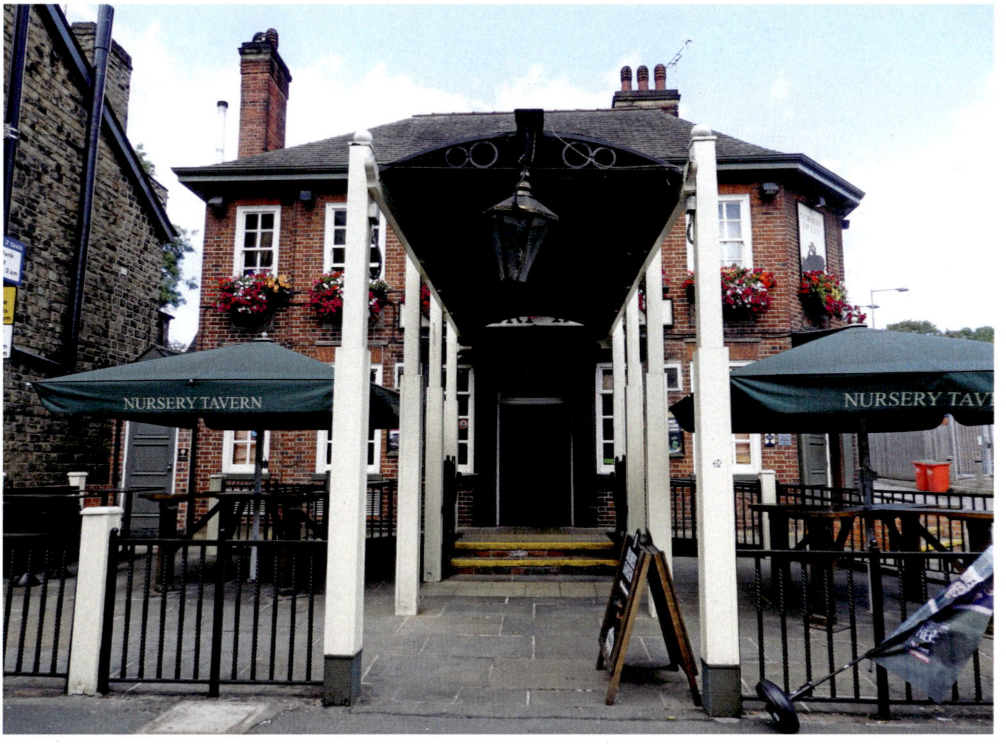

Above: The Nursery Tavern on Ecclesall Road.

Below: The Nursery Tavern's bar.

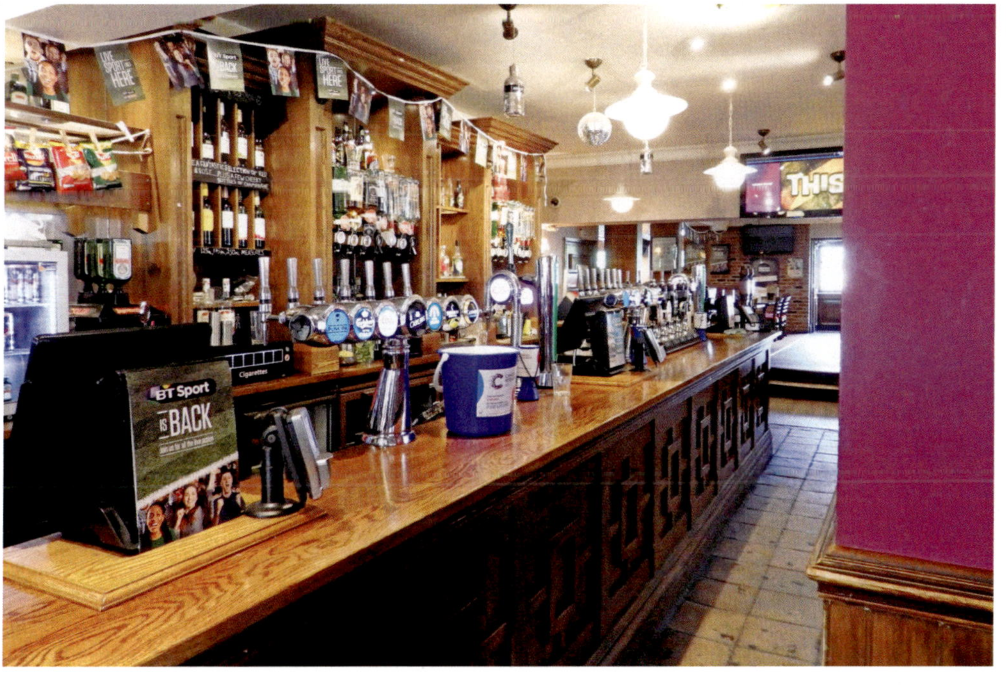

knick-knacks and antiques collected by the somewhat formidable landlady, Mrs Vera Jenkins. This amazing lady celebrated her 82nd birthday by pulling pints and, in February 1986, announced that she was to retire. This brought to a close over fifty years' of association with the Nursery Tavern. She had learnt her trade from her father Fred Hurst when he was publican at the Tavern, then took over with her husband George. When he died, Vera carried on the family tradition.

While the pub didn't generally do much food, their hot pork sandwiches were quite famous. When she left the pub, she sold the contents and went to live with her daughter and German son-in-law in a village near Huddersfield. Apparently offered £800 for an antique table, she refused the offer, saying it was too much and asked for £500; they eventually settled on £600. This is a remarkable example of reverse bartering!

This has always been an immensely popular pub, being close to the Collegiate Campus of Sheffield Hallam University and surrounded by student houses for both Sheffield universities. Today, following extensive renovation, the Nursery Tavern offers a wide range of real ales, craft beers and other traditional favourites.

The Old Queen's Head, Pond Hill

Once called 'The Hawle in the Poandes', this historic pub, with one of Sheffield's few remaining Tudor, timber-framed buildings, was the feasting lodge for the great Sheffield Manor Park and located close by the fish ponds and the River Sheaf. Believed to date back to 1475, after serving as the Banqueting House, it may even have been a former wash house for the Sheffield Castle and the Manor Lodge; it was probably this

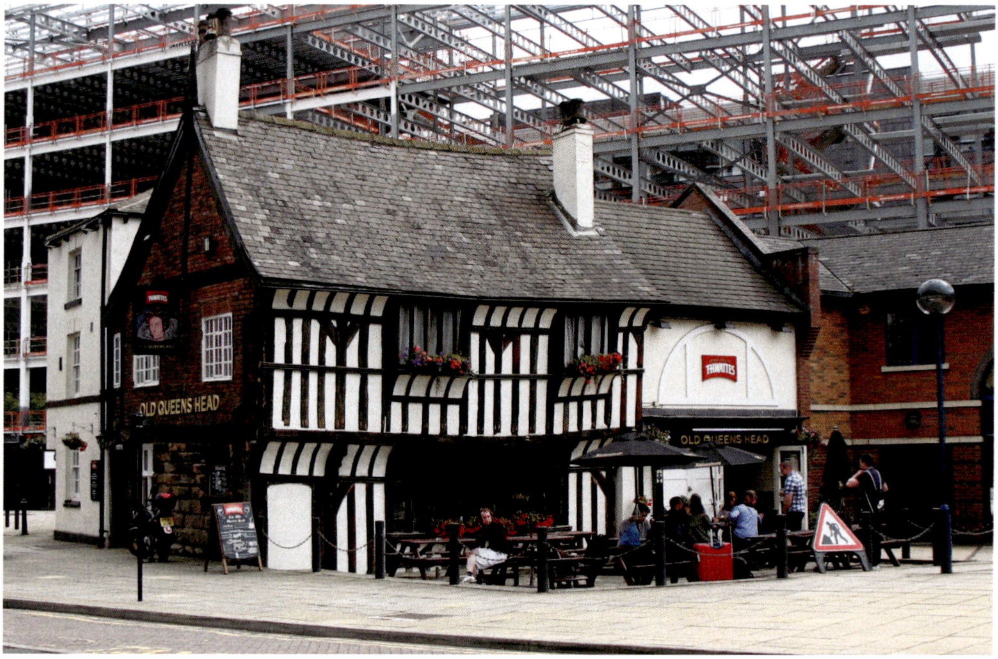

The Old Queen's Head showing the medieval frontage.

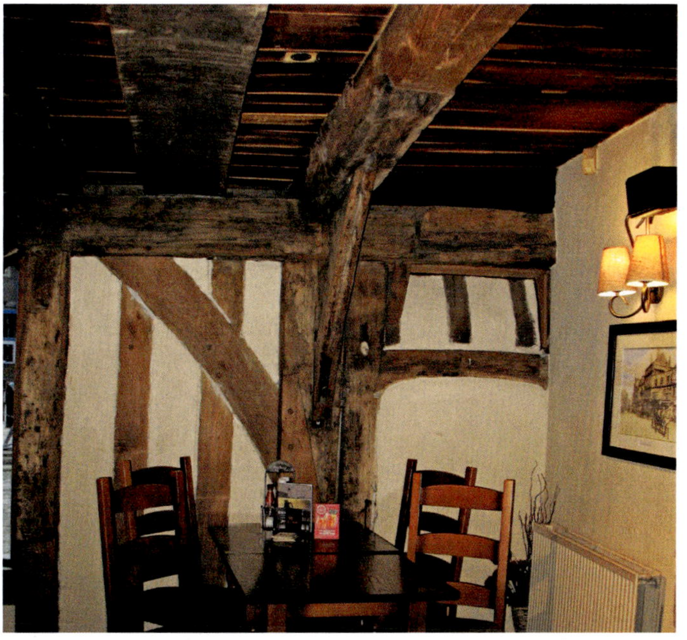

The Old Queen's Head internal building showing framework.

building referred to in an early account book of the Duke of Norfolk's estate – 'the old house in the ponds, formerly wash-house to Sheffield Manor' (17 July 1770). It is suggested that the ponds were originally used for the breeding of carp for the table by the monks of Beauchief Abbey. The monasteries had a monopoly on fish-rearing and, before abolition, fish on a Friday or certain other days of the week and Saints' days meant carp from the fishpond. Somehow the old building survived the expansion of Sheffield's own industrial centre with local forges making use of the water supply. It was used as a residence and the dilapidated structure was acquired in 1842 and turned into a beerhouse by James Pilley, a rivet and nail maker. The original pub opened in the building adjacent to the medieval structure and later extended into the full premises. Pilley paid two guineas licence money to gain approval for the venture. A butter dealer and mason, Joshua Ogden, was resident in part of the building. Much of the local land, including the lease of the Old Queen's Head, was owned by the local brewers, Thomas Rawson. The leasehold passed to Truswell Brewery in 1892, and at that time the premises consisted of a bar, a bar parlour, a taproom, a kitchen, and three bedrooms. By 1884, the ownership had passed to Thomas Berry, then to the Sheffield-based Tennant Brothers brewery, and then to Whitbread. By 1935, the building was owned by Sheffield Corporation and leased to John Smith's Brewery of Tadcaster.

Extensive refurbishment and renovation took place in 1949.This uncovered the original timbers, removing decades of plaster, whitewash, and general grubbiness. The old fireplace was uncovered and stone-mullioned windows were discovered inside the building. Excavations for a new cellar exposed the site of the old well. The building was given Grade II-listed status in 1952 in order to provide some protection for the conservation of this historic site. After further renovations in the late twentieth century and a refurbishment costing around £750,000 by the Tom Cobleigh chain, a steel-encased time capsule was buried in the foundations of the building. The Old Queen's Head is still a popular city-centre establishment for eating and drinking, serving not only traditional English pub food but also a Czech menu. Both can be recommended, with the latter gaining approval from overseas colleagues of two of the authors. The pub is itself a time capsule of Sheffield history, with many old photographs and a display of old artefacts over the ancient stone fireplace. Its setting, tucked around the back of the city's bus station and overshadowed by a new office building, should not deter people from visiting this ancient building. The name may derive from Mary Queen of Scots who was imprisoned in Sheffield from 1570 to 1584.

As with many old taverns, the Old Queen's Head claims its ghostly apparitions, with an elderly man carrying two jugs in his hands. In the 1980s the lady who cleaned at the pub, Audrey Garrett, was apparently terrified of the snug and would call out 'good morning' very loudly, to warn the ghost, before going in to clean. It seemed to do the trick, but despite this, the pub's cats avoided that room...

The Red Lion, Charles Street

Sporting a huge embossed sign on its walls for 'Wards Fine Malt Ales', The Red Lion is a living reminder of a lost heritage of local breweries and of the unacceptable folly of the giant corporations capable of absorbing and then discarding viable local businesses. Today the pub has moved on to become a hugely popular city-centre location for customers from the Hallam University, Science Park, and cultural quarters.

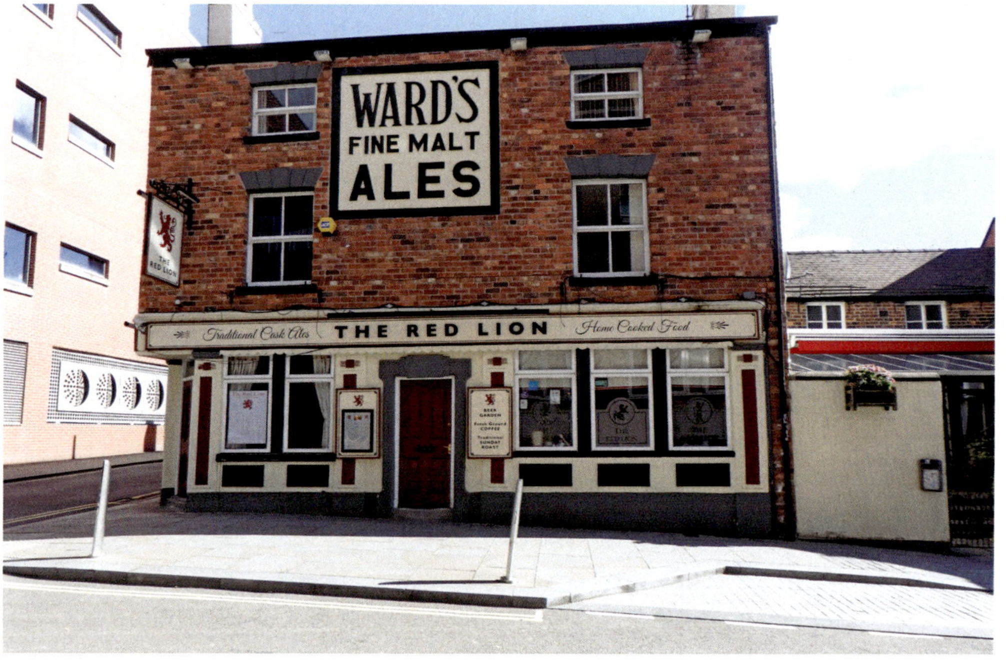

The Red Lion, Charles Street.

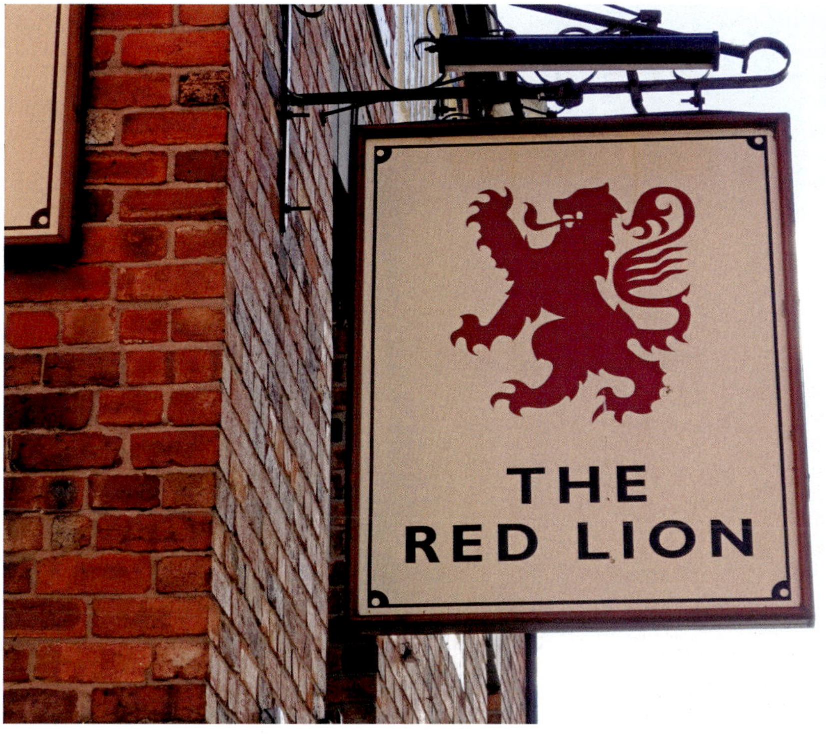

The Red Lion pub sign.

During lunchtime and evenings, particularly post-work, this is a place to escape from a busy world. Now surrounded by modern student residences and refurbished industrial buildings morphed into upmarket city dwellings and retail food outlets, The Red Lion is at the heart of a very vibrant area. The place itself might be described as a good old-fashioned pub, both externally and internally. There is generally a selection of real ales, including some from local breweries and a selection of other drinks. Proximity to the city centre and to the train station, but also little off the beaten track, usually make it a good place for a quiet pint. However, the big screens can be an intrusion on sporting occasions although there is a small conservatory and pleasant pocket-sized pub garden, which is a pleasant place for a pint on summer evenings. They serve food at lunchtime, including Sundays, but not in the evenings. One of the author's has noticed that the recent influx of Chinese students who now live nearby has prompted the pub to advertise their drinks on posters outside the pub in Chinese, an example of local hostelries adapting, as always, to the available market.

The Royal Victoria Hotel, Victoria Station Road

The history of the Royal Victoria Hotel in Sheffield began with the construction of a new red-brick and Pennine Stone building adjacent to the new railway station on the Manchester to Lincolnshire line at the soon-to-be-named Victoria Railway Station. The hotel officially opened by the Sheffield Hotel Co. on 28 July 1862. The owners

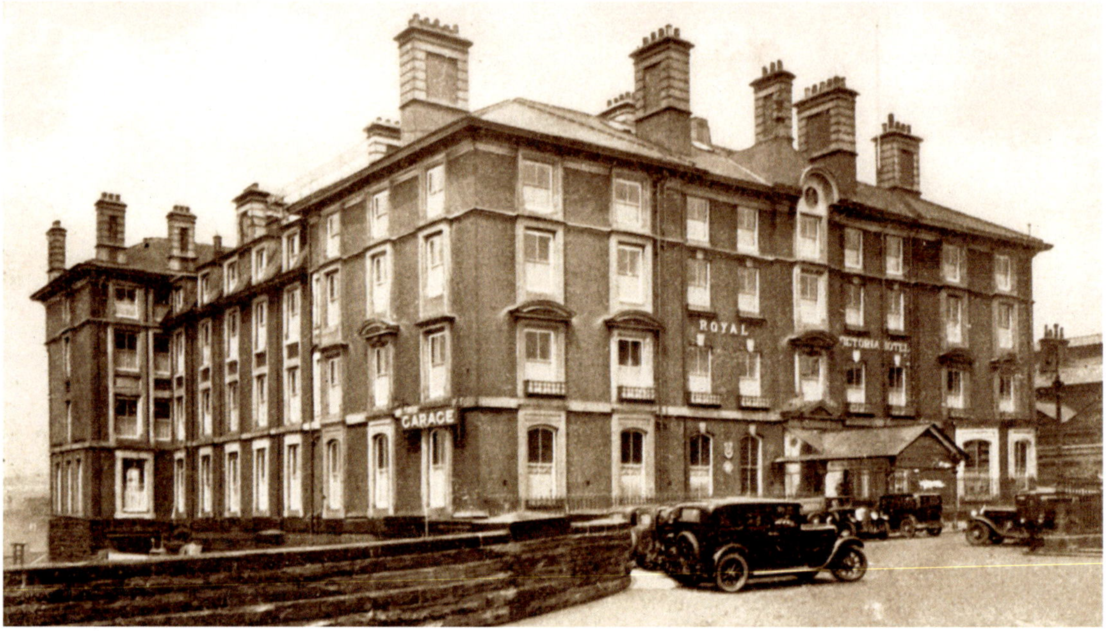

Above: The Royal Victoria Station Hotel, Sheffield, in the early 1900s.

Below: The comfortable interior at the Royal Victoria.

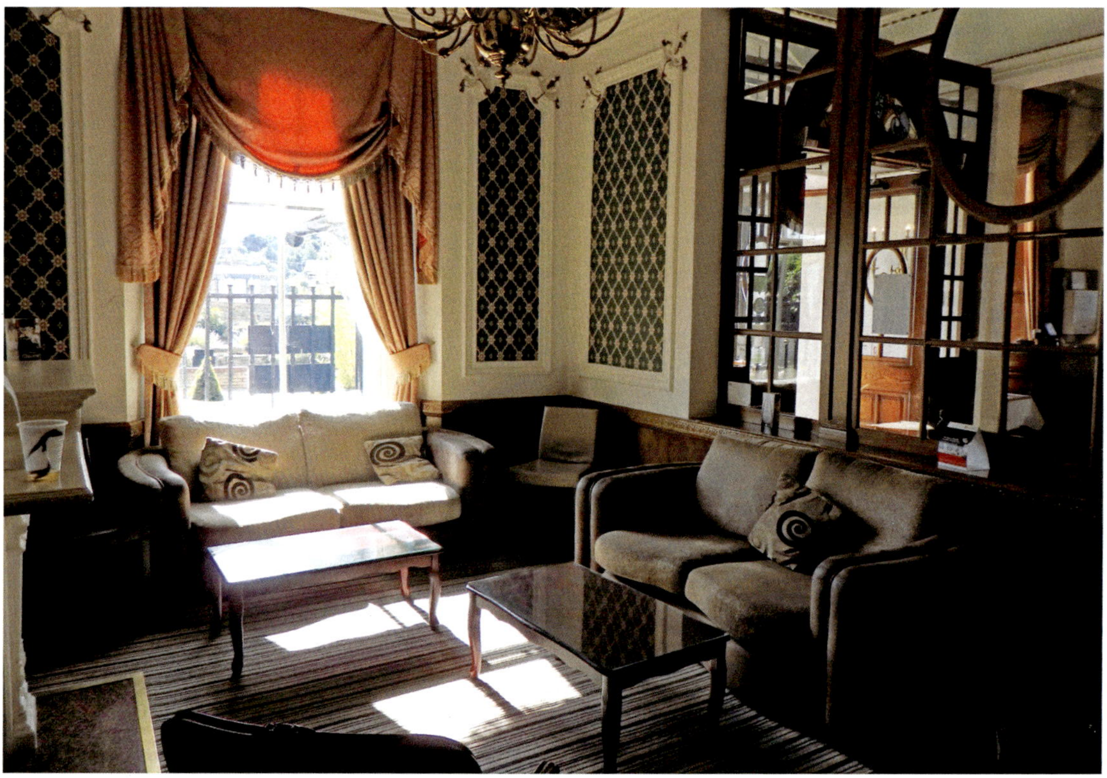

added the 'Royal' prefix following a visit in 1875 by Their Royal Highnesses the Prince and Princess of Wales, later Edward VII and Queen Alexandra. Throughout its history, the hotel has enjoyed royal patronage with visits from Queen Victoria in 1897, and Princesses Elizabeth and Margaret in 1947.

The hotel building itself dates back to 1862, seventeen years after the railway station it was to serve originally opened. John Fowler, who later gained fame for co-designing the Forth Railway Bridge in Scotland, was employed to engineer the extension to the Victoria Station. Fowler's design included a 40-foot high, 750-yard viaduct over the Wicker or the Wicker Arches as they are known locally. This extension was completed in 1847–48 and the Victoria Station officially opened on 15 September 1851. The station closed for passengers in the 1970s, with business transferred to the Sheffield Midland Railway Station but remained open for freight until the 1980s. The approach to the hotel is up a long drive from the River Don to the top of the Wicker Arches viaduct and what was the level of the railway station. Today this driveway may no longer serve its original use but gives a sweeping grand entrance to the hotel.

Michael Liversidge's mother, Joan, worked here as a waitress in the 1940s during the Second World War and told Michael that she had waited on the King and Queen of England; Robert Taylor, famous Hollywood actor; and Louis 'Satchmo' Armstrong, an American trumpeter, composer, singer and occasional actor. Joan related a story that Armstrong threw a cup at a member of staff when he noticed it had a hairline crack in it.

The present Holiday Inn, Royal Victoria Sheffield, offers the comforts expected from a modern hotel, but combined with the character of a Grade II-listed building. There is also a welcoming bar and restaurant with an excellent range of food and drink that is open to the public, so you can just call in and have a nice quiet drink in very elegant surroundings. Today, predominantly a hotel and conferencing venue, the Royal Victoria Hotel was renovated in 2008 and boasts 100 spacious guestrooms. There's an elegant restaurant and a beautiful lounge bar that is still open to the public for a casual drink. Other amenities include a 24-hour fitness centre, plus a business centre and meeting space.

Sheffield Tap, Sheffield Midland Railway Station

This pub is situated within Sheffield's main railway station on Platform 1b, although its main entrance is from Sheaf Street through an unassuming door; in good weather there is some outdoor seating here. It was originally the Sheffield Midland Station's refreshment and dining rooms and opened in 1904. By the 1960s, the rooms were unused and falling into decline. In the 1970s, British Rail, who owned the station, decided to make the refreshment room into a waiting room. They removed some of its ornate features, leaving it a shell of its former self. The Grade II-listed interior of the rest of the building was vandalised and eventually closed up in 1976. The interior was left to decay, with the original ornate plaster ceiling suffering partial collapse due to the leaking roof. In 2008, restoration was finally undertaken to bring the refreshment rooms back to life. Jamie Hawksworth, Jon Holdsworth and their team have made a considerable investment to enable the rooms to be brought back to their original condition.

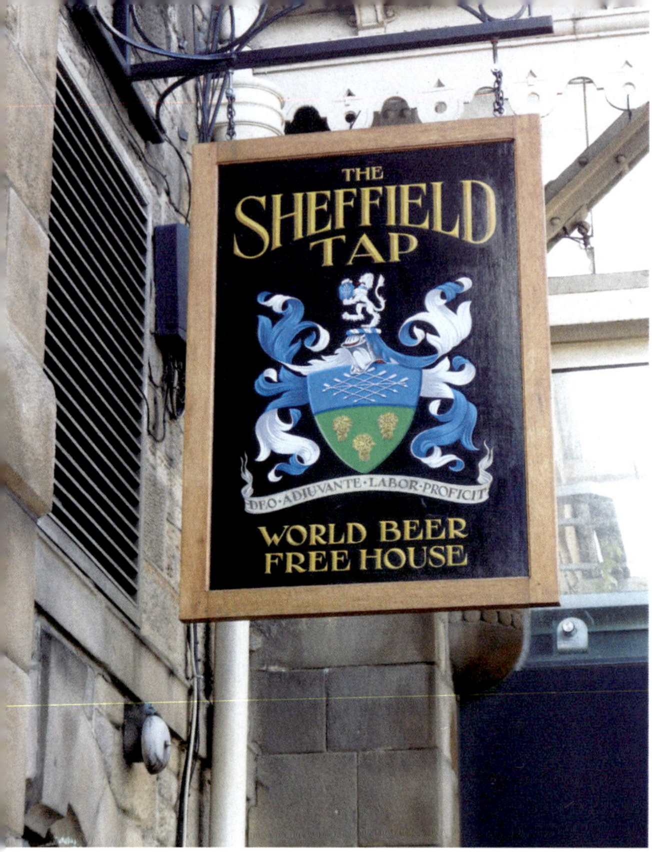

Left: The Sheffield Tap pub sign.

Below: The large bar in the Sheffield Tap.

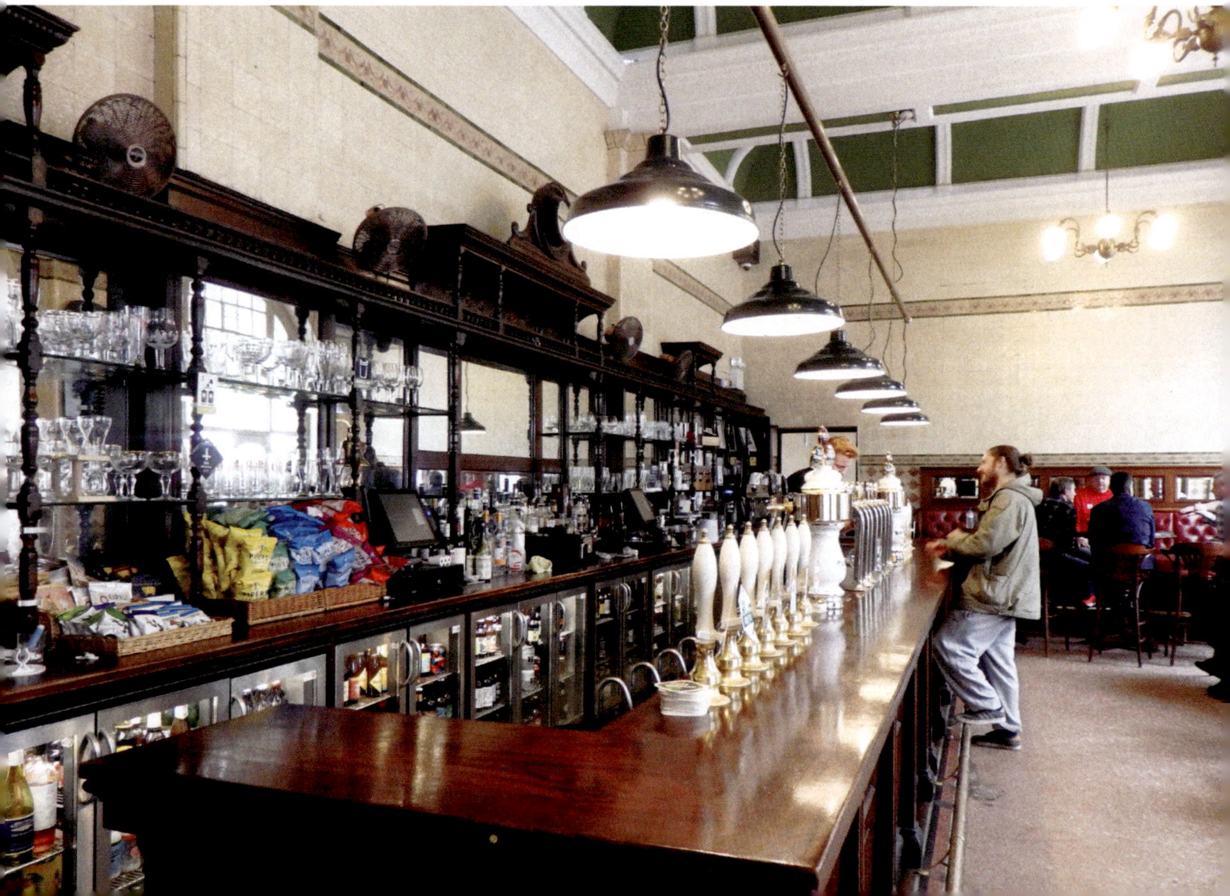

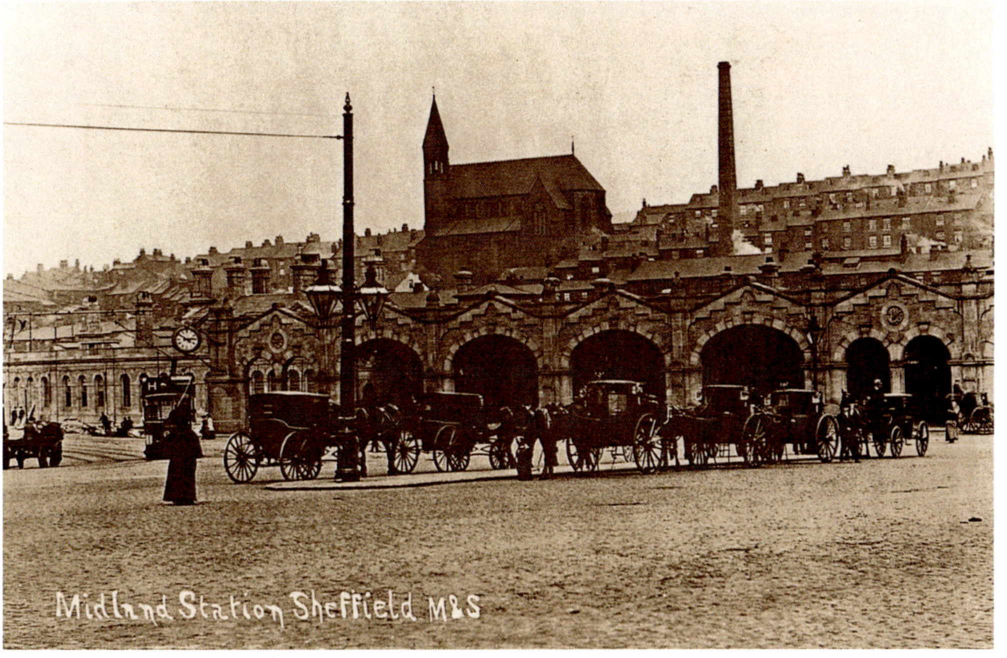

Sheffield Midland Station in the early 1900s.

Work to correct the damage, caused by years of abuse, was undertaken; funded by private investment and a grant from the Railway Heritage Trust. The repair work has been meticulously and thoroughly completed and was given a railway heritage award by CAMRA and English Heritage in recognition of the superb work undertaken. The Sheffield Tap, which opened in 2009, does not serve food but is now a thriving real ale pub with its own small-scale brewhouse on site. It keeps a good selection of cask-conditioned beers and keg beers as well as a huge range of bottled beers from around the world. This pub isn't just a pleasant diversion while waiting for a train but is a destination in its own right. You can not only enjoy a range of interesting beers but also sit in the splendour of the station's Edwardian refreshment rooms. This is a very popular venue for visitors to Sheffield, such as conference goers or simply those passing though by train and awaiting a connection.

The Three Tuns, Silver Street Head

This unusually shaped triangular pub is unique to Sheffield and placed at the junction of two roads in the heart of Sheffield's legal and business quarter. It was recently taken over by the people running the Rutland Arms and the Closed Shop and is a highly recommended pub for good beer and a friendly atmosphere. The site has had a pub on it since at least the early 1800s, as noted in various trade directories, and possibly goes back to the late 1700s. By the 1820s, the landlord was James Staniforth, noted in 1821 as at the Three Tuns in Paradise Square, then in 1822, at No. 7 Silver Street Head, and still there in 1828–29.

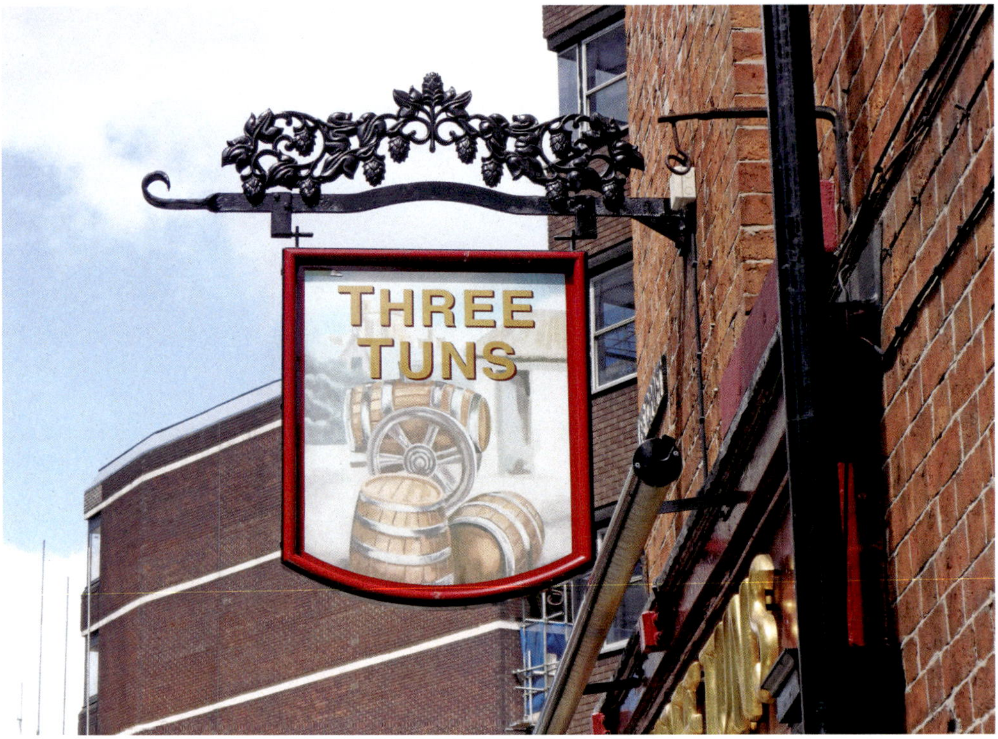

Above: The Three Tuns public house sign.

Below: The imposing building that houses the Three Tuns public house.

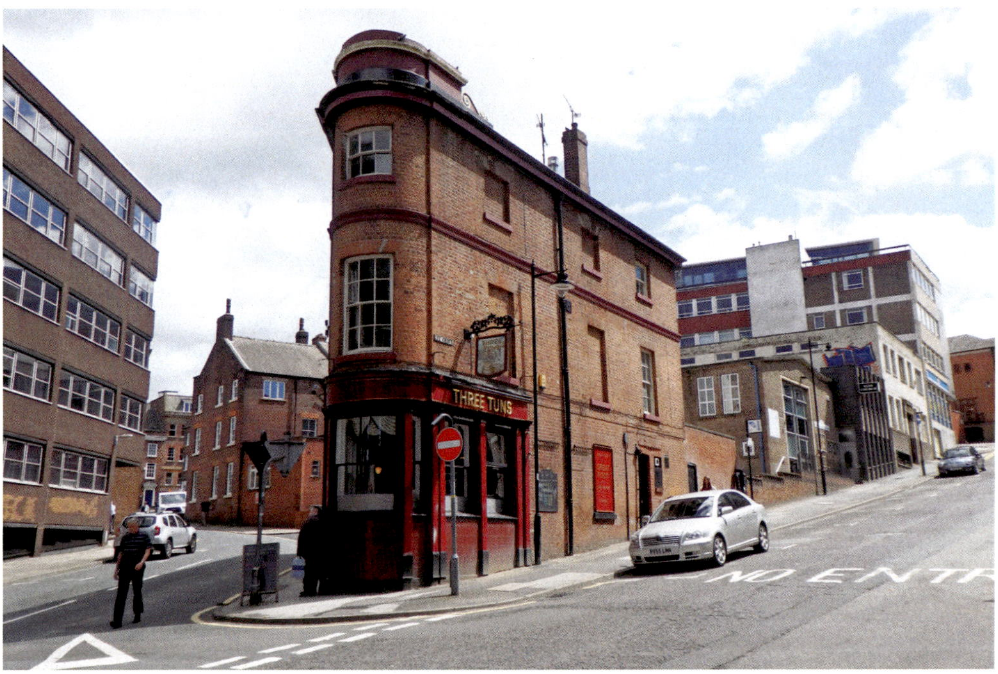

The Three Tuns is set deep in the heart of the legal and professional area of Sheffield. In the 1990s, the premises were earmarked to be transformed into an Irish-themed public house. Thankfully, 1,000 or more persons signed a petition to keep the pub's character and the building was saved. Its exterior cannot now be altered unless it is to enhance the pub. It seems that the Irish-themed idea was not thought through. The 'Tuns' is a highly distinctive building; it has the look of the front of a ship's prow when viewing it from the front. Inside, the pub has a very comfortable feel to it as one of the authors of this book, Michael Liversidge can testify. Mick was not only a regular drinker there but for many years was also a member of the Three Tuns football team.

The main customer base is from the aforementioned legal and professional trade who predominantly work in Paradise Square, which is within a few metres from the Tuns' front door. It is believed that there have been buildings here from around the fifteenth century and some may even have been drinking establishments. Other stories tell that, around the early 1700s, it was a wash house for the St Vincent's Convent, which was sited nearby.

The Three Tuns is a sister pub to the Closed Shop at Commonside, Walkley, and the Rutland near the city centre. It has a long list of great ales and an excellent food range.

The Ship Inn, Shalesmoor

The current pub is part of the Artisan Tap group spread across the region, which offers between them over forty different artisan beers. It is recorded in the 1852 edition of White's Directory of Sheffield with W. Ibbotson as the landlord. By 1879, the pub had changed hands with William Pattinson, the landlord until 1881. He was described as a widower of Barlborough. His family are also listed in the directory with his son George (a waiter) and his daughter Ada, together with a housekeeper, Lydia Smith, and a general servant, Helen Hinds. By 1911, the landlord was Frederick Rogers, and then George Herring by 1919.

This public house has survived several traumas, such as the 'Great Sheffield Flood' caused by the Dale Dyke Dam bursting in 1864. On 11 March 1864, the dam burst its walls and the flood overwhelmed great swathes of low-lying Sheffield. It left 240 people dead in its wake. Two of the victims, both men, were said to have been lodging in the Ship at that time and a plaque outside the pub relates the event, stating that no bodies were ever recovered. An alternative tale relates that the two men, both sailors, drowned in an underground tunnel that connected the pub to the old Ball Bridge Wharf. The tunnel was used for transferring liquor to the pub and the two sailors got caught out as they went about their business. One of the men, we believe, was named Charlie and it is he, supposedly, who stalks the pub late at night as a ghostly apparition. One wonders why it is not during the afternoon or early evening when customers could witness this spectral visitation. Or is that a sceptical response?

The Ship Inn was built around the 1820s and is one of the most striking public houses in Sheffield, with its beautifully tiled exterior and recently refurbished interior that has been preserved with its restored original features; it really does make it a pleasure to have a pint within its portals. It is situated in the Kelham Island quarter of Sheffield and offers the delights of real and craft ale, freshly brewed coffee, artisan

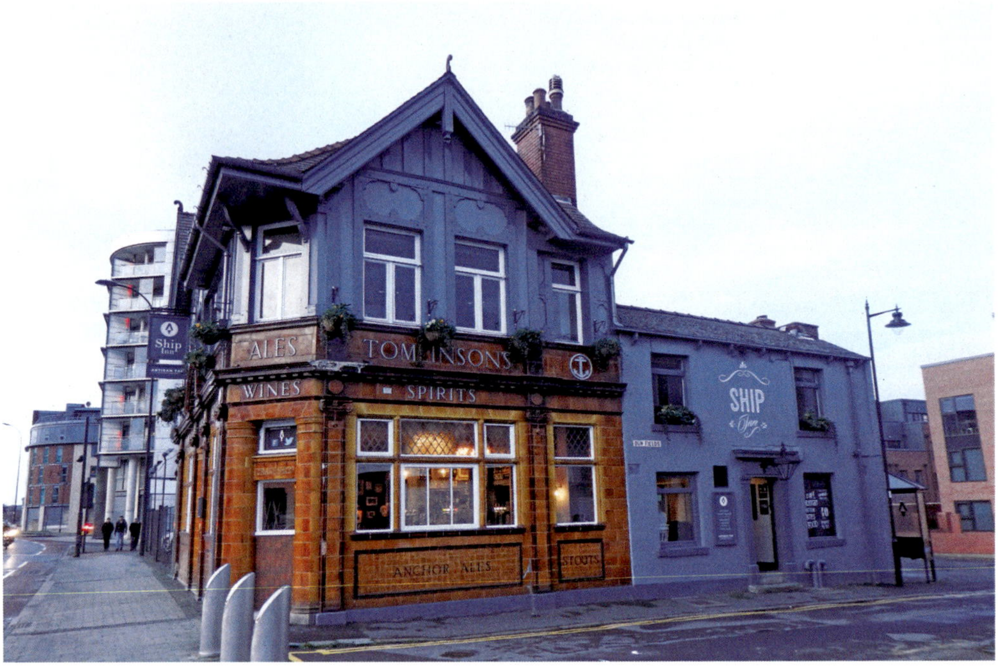

Above: The ornate, tiled exterior of the Ship Inn.

Below: The bar area in the Ship Inn.

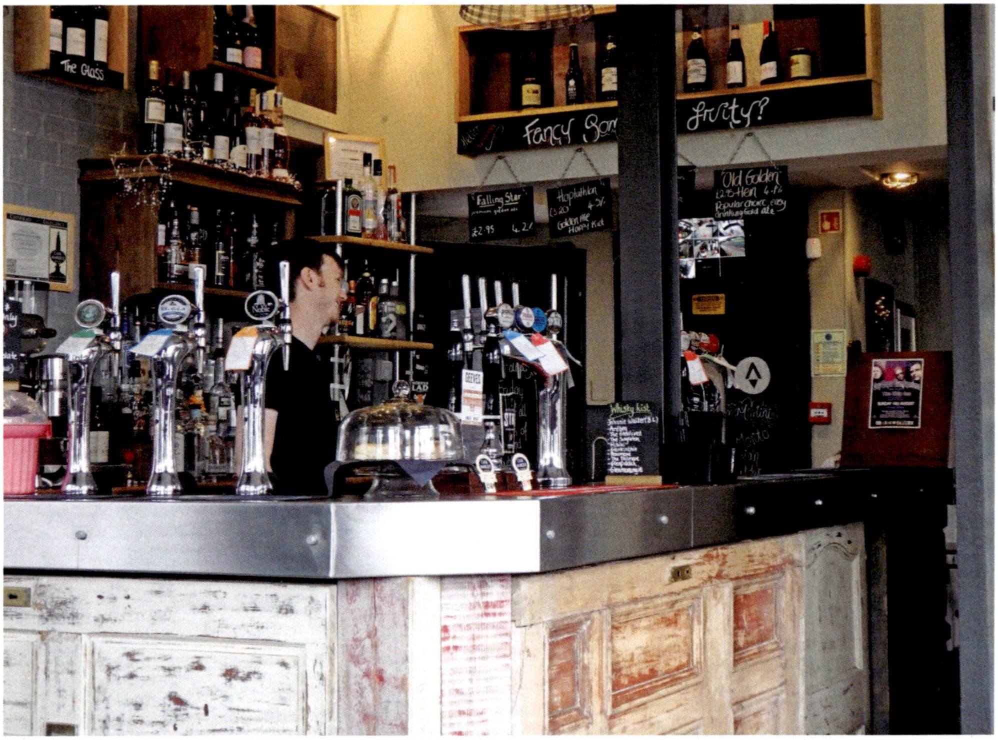

snacks, free Wi-Fi and a fresh modern twist. Owners, Hawthorn Leisure, recognised the importance of reviving the Ship Inn with her history and pride of place in Kelham Island, and injected a sizeable cash investment. Many of the original features of the pub have been retained, including the unique brown tiles on the outside and restoration of the original tiling on the inside, which builders found hidden beneath decades of paint. The name 'Ship Inn' may derive from a sailing ship and the proximity to the local wharf but traditionally it was an alternative pub name for Noah's Ark, used to avoid any religious connotations.

The Ship Inn is now a well-lit, spacious venue filled with the history of a traditional pub and the comforts of a modern pub. Drinkers and diners can relax in the retro 1960s armchairs while admiring artwork showing the history of Sheffield and deciding what to savour from the extensive list of craft beers, cask ales, wines and spirits.

Chapter Two

From Grenoside and North-East Sheffield to the Lower Don Valley, Attercliffe and Darnall

Acorn Inn, Bracken Hill, Burncross

The Acorn Inn at Burncross is a long-established pub with a considerable history. It celebrated its 150th anniversary in October 2008 with a family fun day. This event was attended by then Lord Mayor, Cllr Jane Bird and Sheffield Wednesday footballers

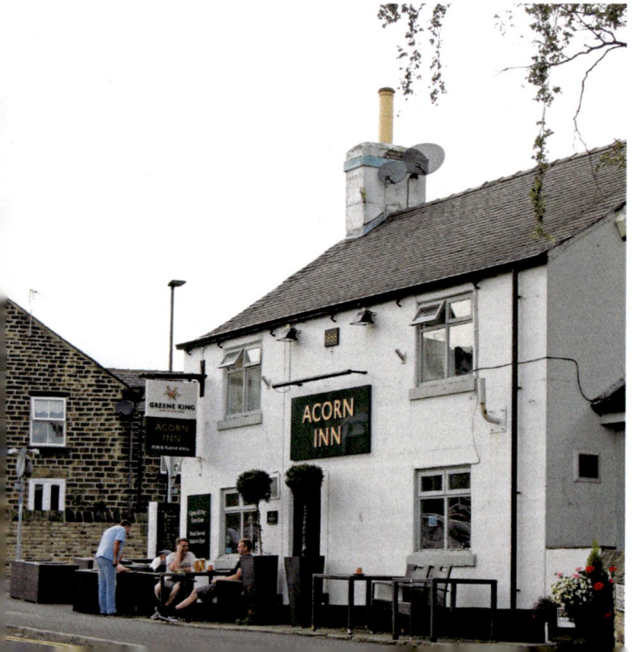

The Acorn Inn looking towards Hollow Gate. Note the date stone on the building.

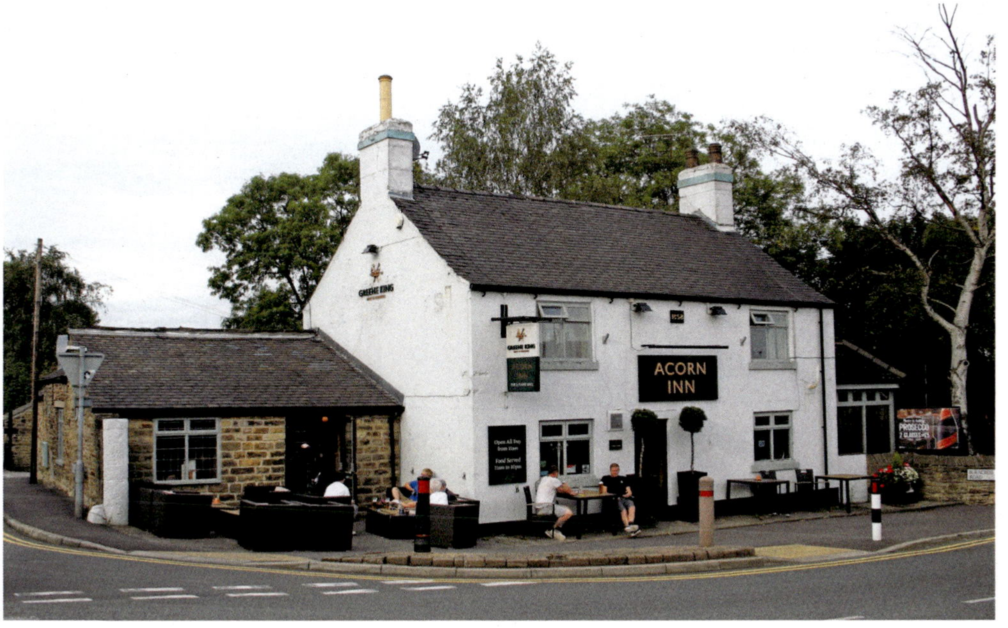

The Acorn Inn, showing the different buildings that make up the modern pub.

Sean McAllister and Akpo Sodje. There is a date stone on the front of the main pub building of 1858 when the landlord was Thomas Chapman. It started life as a beerhouse half-way up Bracken Hill in the early nineteenth century when William Beighton was the landlord. The pub now sits at the crossroads at the bottom of Bracken Hill on the corner of Burncross Road and Hollowgate.

It first opened as a beerhouse with the landlord recorded as also working as a file-cutter, a common trade in the area. By 1889, Albert Walton had become the landlord, describing himself as 'victualler', already providing food. The outline of the original cottage and outbuildings that housed the pub can still be seen, although the pub has been modernised and includes an outside seating area fronting on Burncross Road and a pub garden with children's play area to the side. The pub is presently part of the Greene King brewery chain with Cask Marque ales. It is a popular meeting place with local people, serving a range of beers and meals. It is one of the local pubs that take part in the annual Burncross Beer Festival. The name 'Acorn' may be derived from an association with the Oak Tree, a common pub name.

Arena Square, Attercliffe Common

Arena Square is a Table Table establishment that serves meals – very nice ones too – throughout the day. This very large public house was built by Whitbread in 1998 and became the first, new licensed premises to be built on Attercliffe Common for over eighty years. The pub-come-restaurant was built at a time when the steel industry that had made this part of Sheffield thrive was in decline. Whitbread must be given some credit for taking such a risk, although by then the redevelopment of the area was well

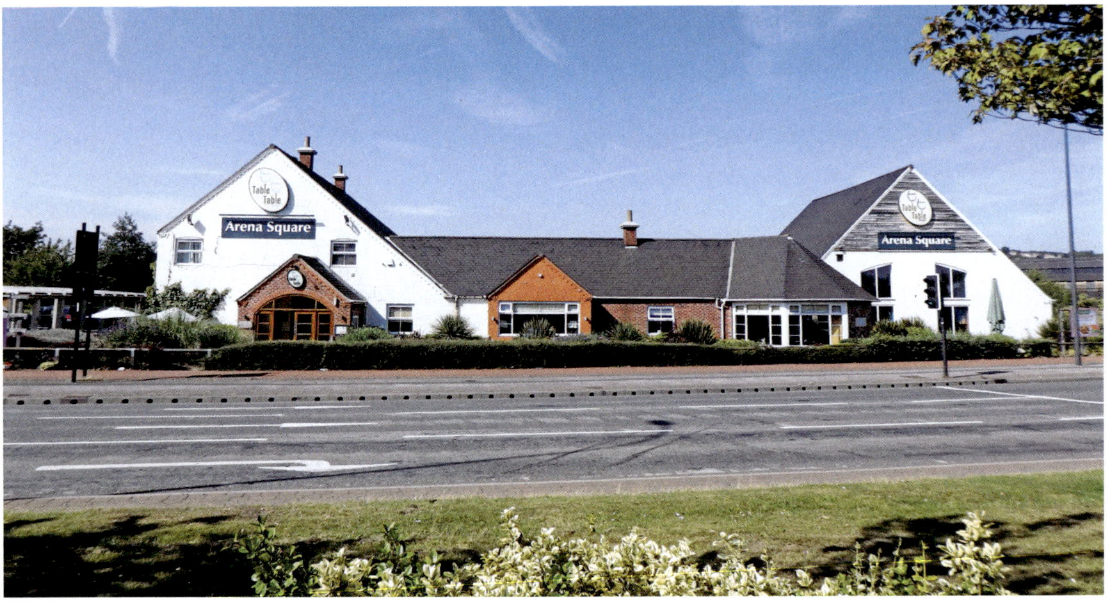

Above: Arena Square.

Below: Arena Square's bar area.

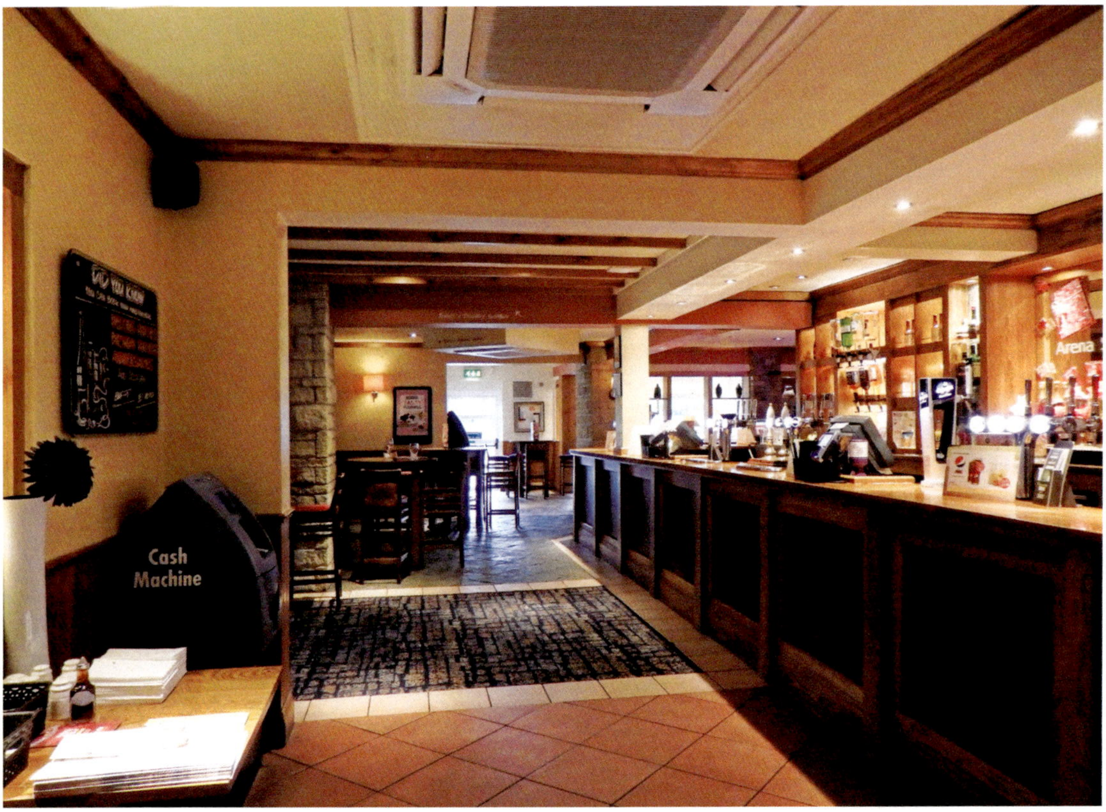

underway with nearby retail and sporting facilities already built. The pub itself is still flourishing, benefitting from its proximity to Sheffield Centertainment (which houses 20 cinemas, around ten restaurants, indoor golf, a children's play area, an amusement arcade, laser quest and tenpin bowling), which is just a few hundred yards away. The overspill from the tens of thousands of people who visit the centre every single day helps the Arena Square immeasurably.

The public house was given its name following a competition in the local Sheffield newspaper, *The Star*. The Arena Square was selected from thousands of entries received by Whitbreads Brewery. It is situated on Attercliffe Common by the side of the famous Sheffield Forgemasters, across the road from the Motorpoint Arena Sheffield and iceSheffield. Many big name bands, singers and comedians perform at the Motorpoint and this also gives the Arena Square plenty of extra custom.

The atmosphere at the restaurant is unbeatable and, with their menu of freshly cooked pub classics and friendly and experienced team, is a pub that is well worth a visit!

Carbrook Hall, Carbrook Road, Attercliffe

Another example of a very old building turned into a hostelry and still going strong is Carbrook Hall. The 'Carbrook' as it is known to the locals is a friendly public house with a real feel of history to it. When you go through the door and into the main room or dining area it is like being transported back hundreds of years – the fully oak carved wall panelling and the carved oak fireplace are real things of beauty. There is even a suit of armour standing in the corner. It is believed that the site has had human

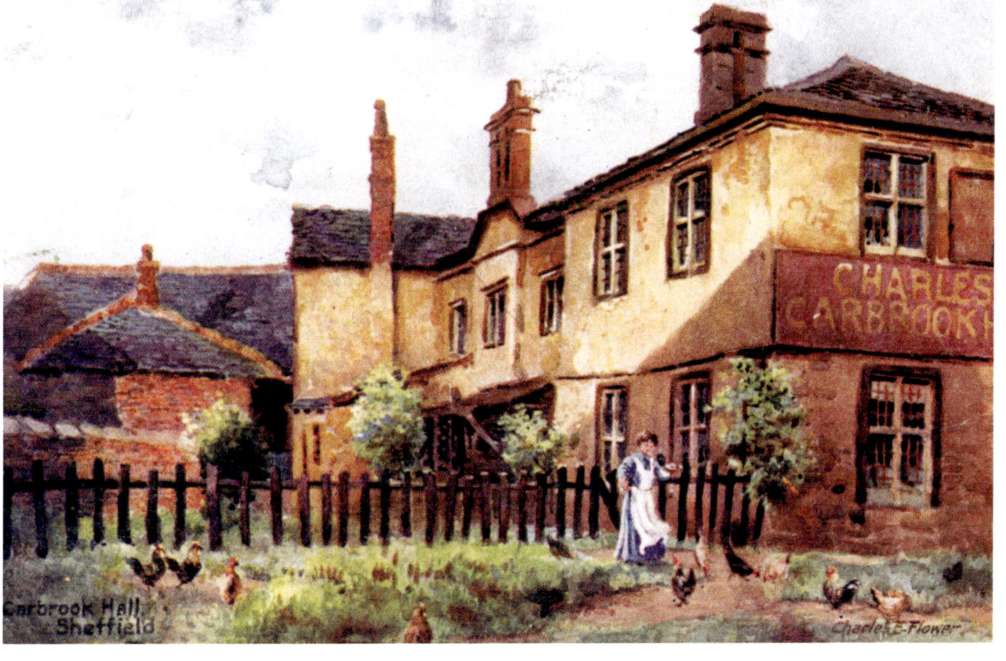

Old Carbrook Hall, Attercliffe, in the 1800s.

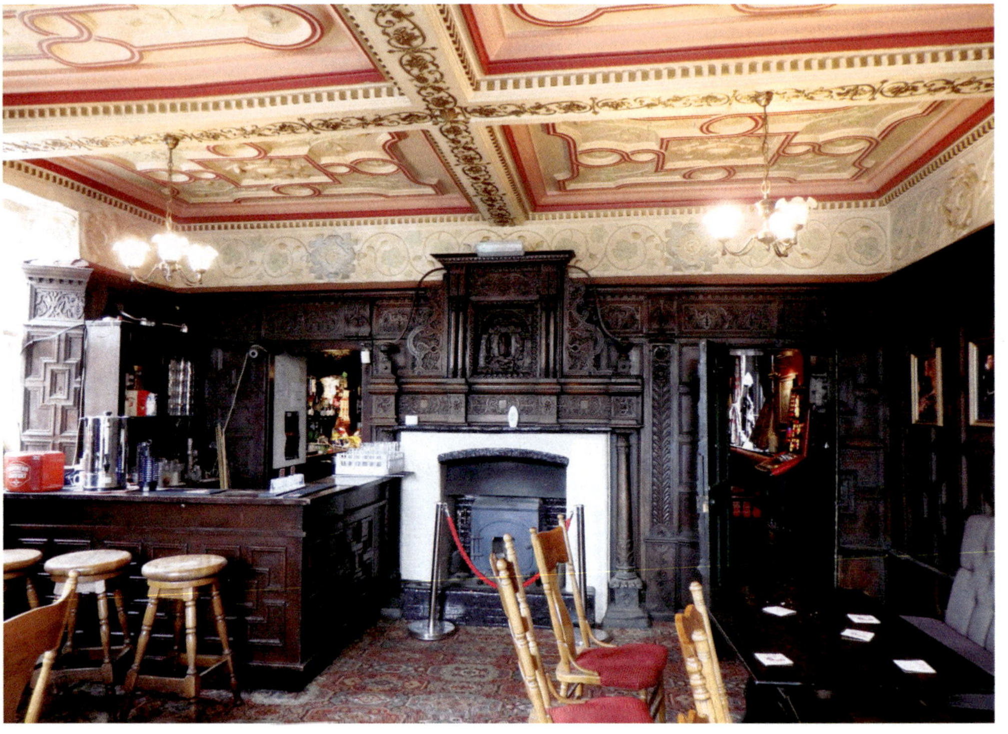

Carbrook Hall's ornate carved room.

habitation as far back as around 1176, at which time it was owned by the Blunt family. Even the present-day building takes us back to a time when the industrial Lower Don Valley was a rural idyll. The place is steeped in history with, for example, the Bright family, significant in the English Civil War (1642–49), being residents here. Col John Bright of the Parliamentary Army was appointed commander of Sheffield Castle after it fell from Royalist hands. Bright later became Governor of York from 1649 to 1660, and High Sheriff of Yorkshire from 1654–55. He was a distinguished military leader and a personal friend of Oliver Cromwell. The Brights had acquired the place after rebuilding in 1462, when Thomas Bright, lord of the manor of Ecclesall, purchased the property. The hall had various residents and owners over the centuries and spent a long period as a farmhouse. By the mid-1800s, Carbrook Hall had become a 'common beerhouse', and in the late twentieth century was restored as the modern Lower Don Valley emerged from its period of declining heavy industry. Renovation revealed and conserved many original features of an earlier building, probably from around 1620. The pub claims to be Sheffield's most haunted, with, it is said, members of the Blunt family, the Brights, and others haunting the place over several centuries. Some people have described a mysterious elderly lady sitting forlornly in an old rocking chair and a dark hooded figure, perhaps a long-dead monk. Others describe glasses unexpectedly thrown off shelves, televisions switched off, drawers dislodged, floating cigarettes with nobody holding them and people grabbed by invisible hands – a typical evening out in the Don Valley perhaps. However, when interviewed for *The Star*, in 1983, the then landlords Keith and Doreen Woodhouse dismissed any such claims and emphasised that they never had any problems with hauntings. However, it is still thought to be 'Sheffield's, if not England's most haunted public house'. John Bright, in his puritan garb, is said to be the most frequently seen apparition. Still, it must be good for business.

Carbrook Hall has stood through many of England's – as well as Sheffield's – historic events. From its early days standing in green open countryside, the place has witnessed the English Civil War, the Industrial Revolution, the 1864 Great Sheffield Flood (when over 240 people lost their lives in England's worst peacetime disaster) and two world wars. The latter included the German blitz of Sheffield in 1940, where the main target was the steel factories that surround the site. This was followed by the slum clearance of Attercliffe in the 1950s, 60s and 70s when nearly all the local residents were moved away from the old houses to more modern council estates. Then, by the 1980s, almost all of the mass labour-intensive steel industry had closed. Despite all of these, today the pub is a well-known and popular location for good beer, decent food, and with access to a variety of entertainment, including the nearby Centertainment complex, and is of course at the heart of the Don Valley sports, retail and entertainments area. The future looks bright for a hostelry such as this, with the economic resurgence of business in the immediate area and huge numbers of tourism visitors to events, activities, and retail leisure.

The Old Harrow, Main Street, Grenoside

The Old Harrow is a warm and friendly pub, currently part of the Enterprise Inns chain, which provides good food (including locally sourced meat) and drink at reasonable prices. This historic tavern is located in the middle of Grenoside village, itself of great charm and interesting heritage. The story of the Old Harrow began after the parliamentary Inclosure Act of 1789, through which local man Matthew Ellison was awarded a rood (just over a quarter of an acre) and five perches (around $5^{1}/_{2}$ yards) of land to the west of the new Sheffield to Halifax Turnpike road. The cost to Ellison was only £9.00, but that was then a large sum of money (for example, a worker's wages for the week would be about two shillings, with twenty shillings to one pound). With the land came a cottage and Matthew Ellison was noted as the innkeeper. Interestingly though, it was not until 1802 that the 'cottage' was described as a public house – at which point it was called 'The Sign of the Harrow'. Matthew Ellison is believed to have died soon after acquiring the land and getting the pub established, leaving his property to four children: Sarah, Elizabeth, David and George. However, Sarah died in 1796 and was followed soon by her sister, Elisabeth in 1800. One of the sons, George, subsequently (in 1802) bought out the share in the property of his brother David. It seems that fatalities were happening speedily at this point and George passed away in 1804, leaving the property to his two daughters, Ann and Mary. Following their inheritance, Ann married Joseph Haigh and Mary married Joseph Woodhead. The latter purchased Haigh's share of the tavern in 1823 and, when he died, they passed to Benjamin Woodhead, who is presumed to be his son. Benjamin sold the Harrow

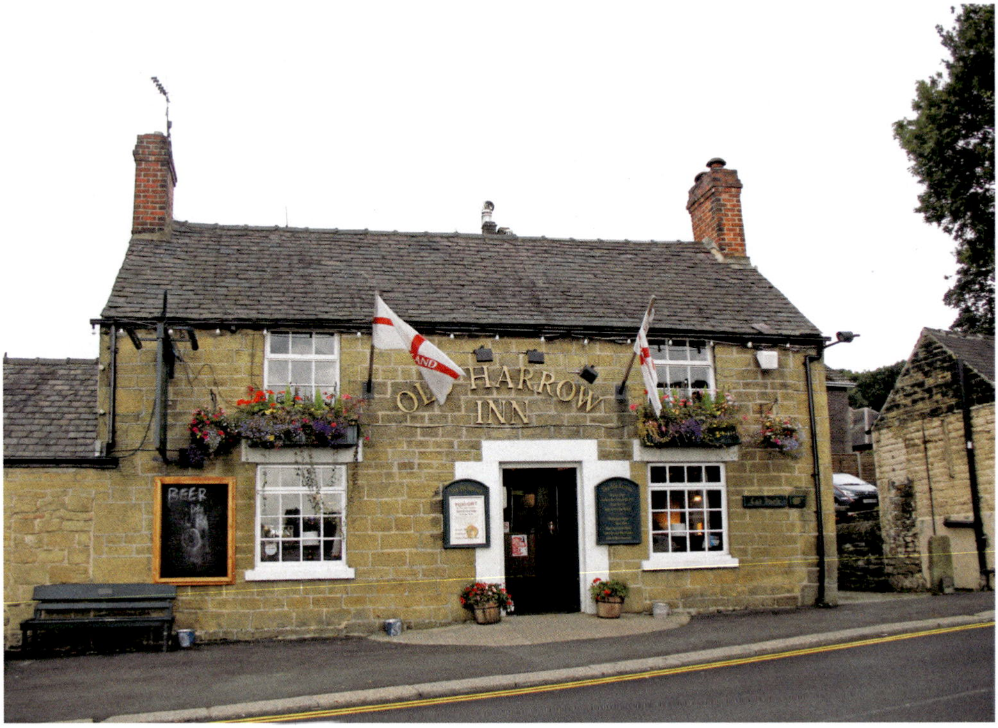

Old Harrow's frontage onto Main Street.

in 1849 to George and William Walker Smith. The original cottage was incorporated into the new pub buildings as the premises were modified and extended throughout this period. The Woodheads and the Smiths did not actually run the pub but let the tenancy to Mary Turner in 1825, and to William Croft by 1833. The latter was also a butcher, something we note elsewhere as pub landlords often had a number of business interests. In 1841, stone mason James Gillot was the landlord, followed in 1852 by Thomas Lint from Cudworth. Later publicans included Henry Beaver in 1861 and Edward Morrison in 1871, the latter also running a horse bus service between Grenoside village and Sheffield. It seems that by 1881 the landlord was Nancy Nuttall but she had left by 1884 when William Kirk became landlord. In White's Trade Directory of 1889, Thomas Nightingale is listed as a victualler at what has now become 'the Old Harrow'. He was followed by local bus proprietor William Heaps. A lasting legacy from this gentleman was the corner of the road at Main Street and Stephen Lane, which was known as 'Heaps' Corner'. When he died in 1898 his son-in-law, Tom Wasteney, became landlord, but this was short-lived as he passed away in 1901. Phyllis, William Heaps' daughter, then became landlord and when she remarried her new husband ran the pub until his death in 1925.

It is said that during the late nineteenth and early twentieth centuries The Old Harrow, with its bowling green, a knur and spell team and a room upstairs for dancing, was the most popular pub in Grenoside. The Sheffield Don Brewery acquired the pub in 1906 and was taken over by Tennant Brothers in 1916. The pub was extended in the early 1980s into an adjacent shop, thus creating several small rooms. As has been the case for a long time now, the Grenoside Sword Dancers traditionally dance outside the pub on Boxing Day. Either the Old Harrow or the 'Top' Red Lion are the venues for singers and musicians to gather to sing local carols to traditional tunes during December. The Old Harrow is a pub steeped in tradition, which is still offering great hospitality.

The Pack Horse, Pack Horse Lane, High Green

The pub name comes from the medieval and later carriers, 'pack-men', with their strings of packhorses and ponies that transported goods across the countryside in panniers on their backs. They were able to deal with the narrow routes and poorly maintained trackways across sometimes wild countryside and moorland. The pub stands on what is still a no-through road, which peters out to a public-right-of-way footpath, so it is tempting to imagine that both the name of the pub and the lane commemorate one of the old routes down which the packhorse trains moved.

This is a traditionally built small public house serving a range of beers and with a children's playground and beer garden to one side. It caters for passing trade, with a

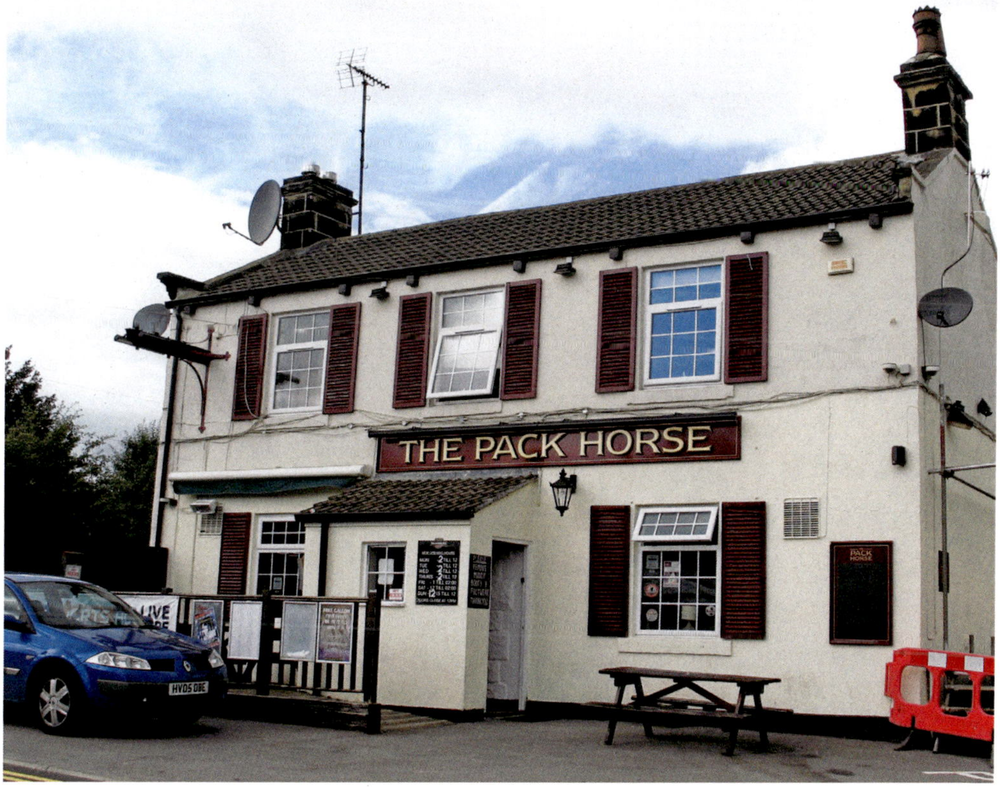

The Pack Horse, showing the entrance porch and the old doorway.

sign outside asking walkers to remove their muddy boots before entering, as well as local people. During the 1970s the landlord held fun days at Easter, which included cake decorating competitions. This tradition of being family oriented continues but it also caters for sports lovers with satellite television.

The Pack Horse is one of only a few remaining pubs in the Mortomley area of High Green. In the nineteenth and for much of the twentieth century, it served the increasing population of miners and foundry workers who worked nearby. In 1889, White's Trade Directory shows that Amos Rodgers was the landlord, described as a victualler. Like many old public houses and taverns, the Pack Horse is reputed to be haunted with people noting 'a presence' in a corner of a room, as well as in the cellar.

The Wentworth House Hotel, Milford Street

On what is left of Milford Street you will find the Wentworth House Hotel, a small unassuming, survivor of a public house next to a Firth Rixon entrance and in the shadow of the Sheffield Forgemasters. Years ago that entrance would have belonged to the English Steel Corporation before it became British Steel. This company was established in 1983 from the merger of Firth Brown and British Steel Corporation's River Don Works forging operations as a public company. These companies were where the Wentworth's main customer base came from for many decades. The shift workers, the '6 am till 2 pm' and the '2 pm till 10 pm' men, used to empty out of the steelworks with a thirst to quench. Plenty of the pubs in this vicinity of the steelworks stayed open past their legal closing time to accommodate the thirsty visitors. They also picked up workers who would be having a drink, or two before going on to work, especially the '10 pm till 6 am' night shift – not exactly politically correct or health and safety conscious. The Wentworth bar staff would be pulling the pints and line them up along

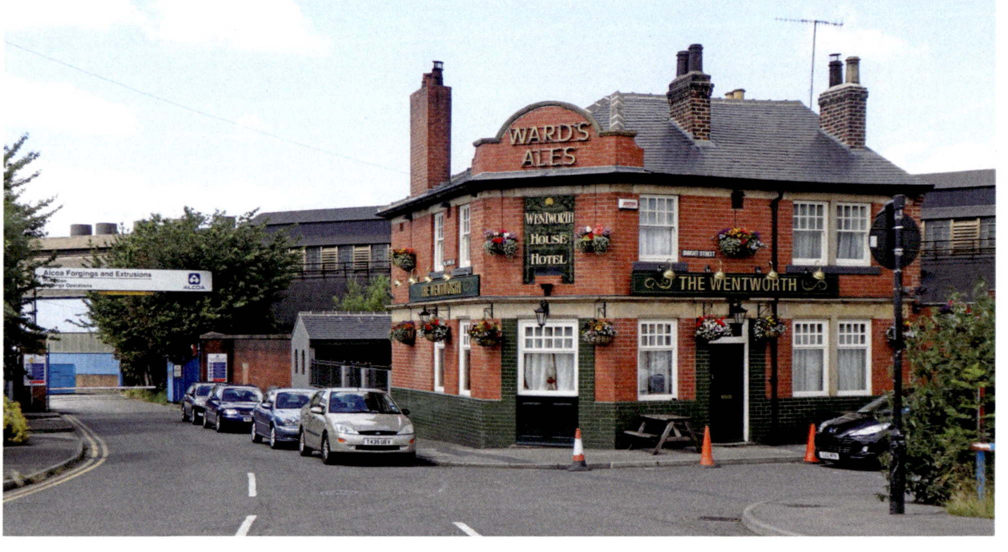

The beautiful red-brick and tiled exterior of the Wentworth House Hotel.

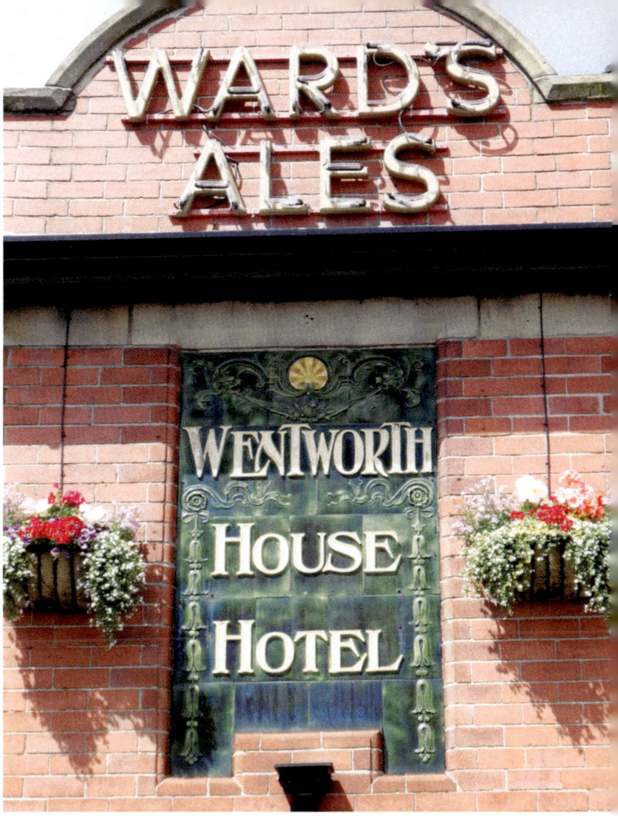

Right: Pub sign of the Wentworth House Hotel.

Below: The Wentworth House Hotel smokers' sheltered area with its metal cigarette advertisements.

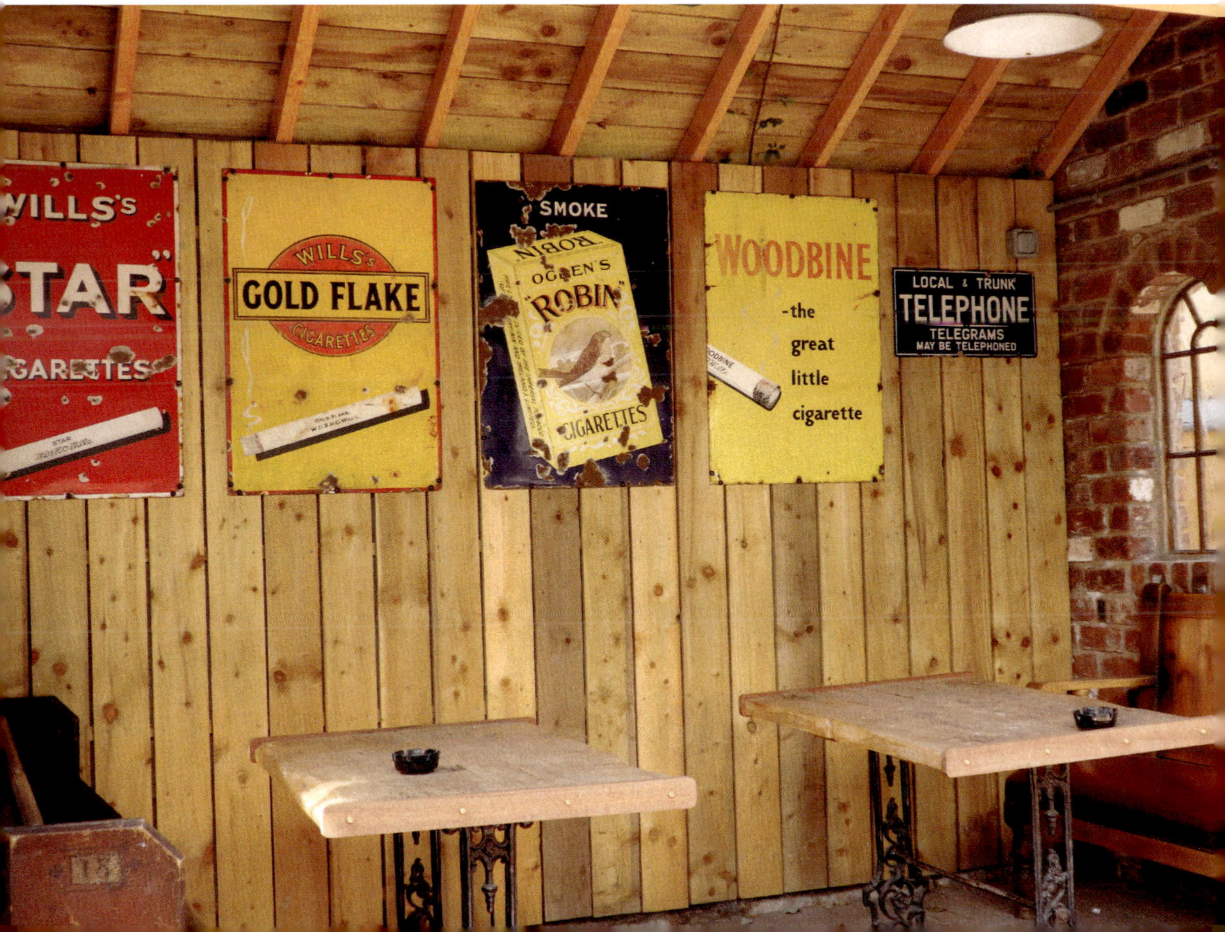

the bar so the men would come in, grab their pints and just sit down. Payment would be made later before they headed for home, a trusting and familiar format of hospitality.

The Wentworth House Hotel was a beer-only house until 1979 when it was refurbished and granted a full license. This was quite a while after the Attercliffe slum clearances, which happened in the late 1960s and early 1970s, left this public house forlornly fighting for its life when almost forty other public houses in the very close proximity all ceased trading. The few remaining Attercliffe valley pubs at that time only survived through local drinkers revisiting their old stomping ground. All the surrounding houses were demolished, as previously stated, by the mid-1970s and no real effort was made to develop this area for almost twenty years until the Supertram track was laid to go through Attercliffe on its way to Meadowhall Shopping Centre and Centertainment, which houses a 20-cinema complex and around a dozen restaurants opened in about 1993. The Wentworth has stood out with its resilience and determination to survive. It also stands out in the darker winter evenings when it is viewed with its wonderfully tiled frontage strategically illuminated. It is, perhaps, the most dramatic of public houses in Sheffield – long may it survive.

The White Rose, Handsworth Road, Darnall

The name of this pub is a common one, commemorating the emblem of Yorkshire and the Yorkist dynasty of English kings, including Richard III. At one time, there was another White Rose nearby in Darnall but this is no longer a pub. This White Rose, on

The White Rose.

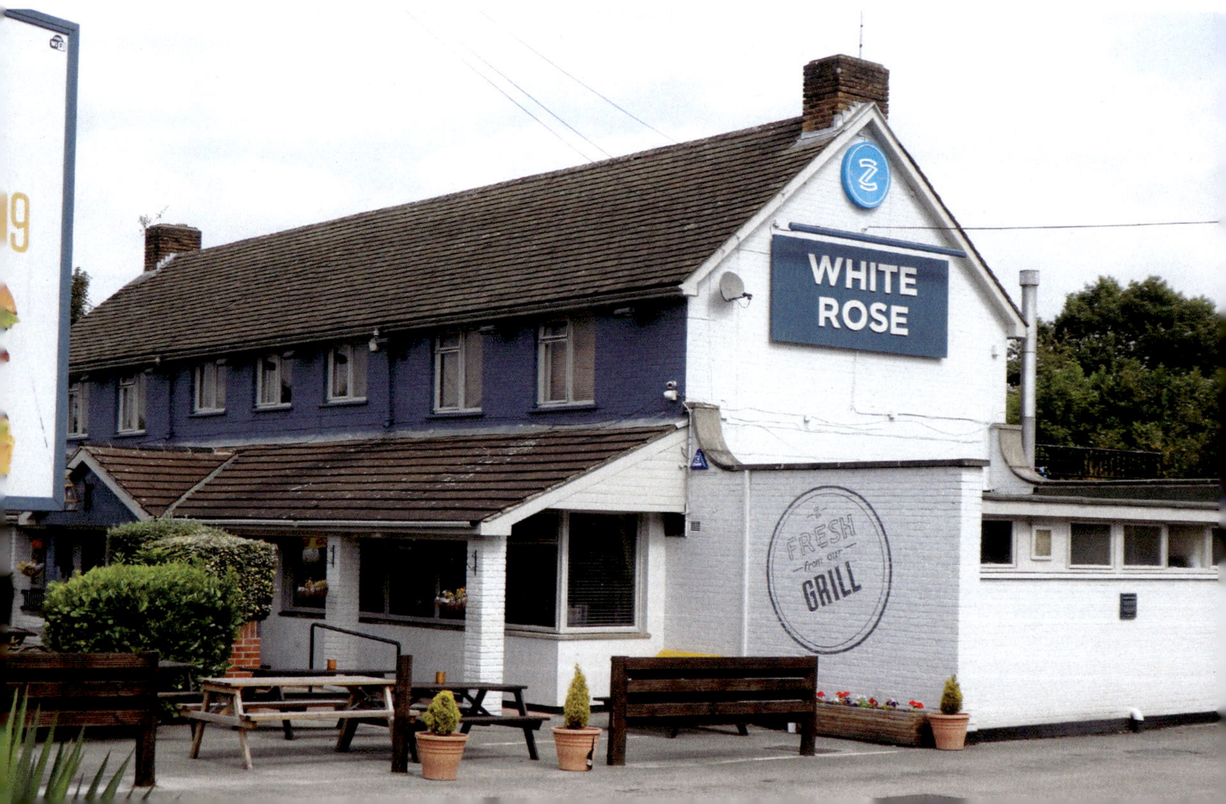

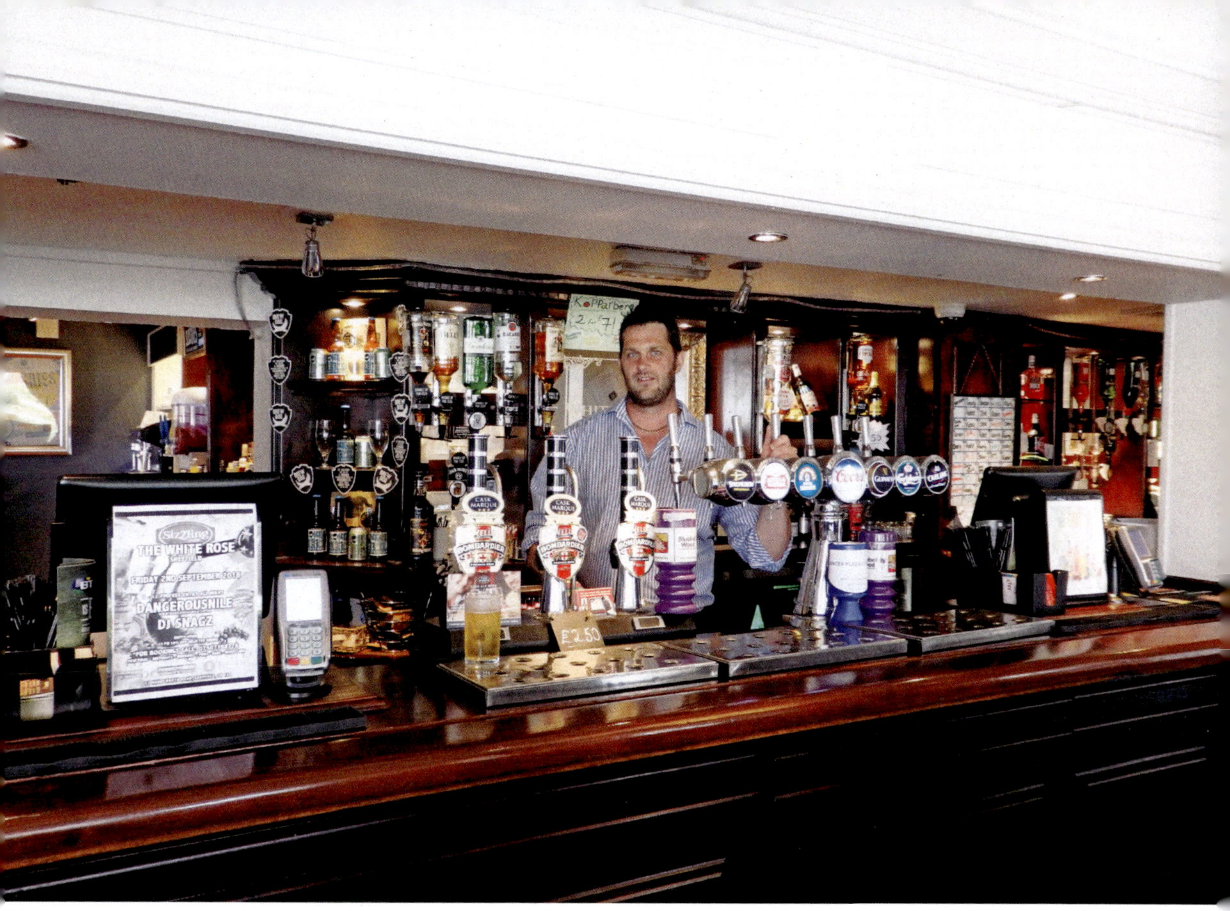

The White Rose manager, Simon, at the bar in the White Rose.

Handsworth Road, is a large purpose-built pub dating from the mid-twentieth century. Its style reflects this with two large rooms and windows to match with a restaurant area to the rear. It not only has a large car park but also a seating area at the front of the pub, popular with diners and drinkers alike. One of the authors remembers this pub from the mid-1970s as extremely popular for dining, seen as an alternative to the 'Berni Inn' chain with the restaurant area used for private functions. (For those younger readers, the Berni's were almost the first of the hugely popular steakhouse chains of pubs and inns and, in the 1960s or 1970s, seemed the height of modern sophistication; completed with After Eight mints served with the coffees. The Norton at Meadowhead in south Sheffield was one of the first 'Berni's'. The Berni chain was later followed by the Toby Inns and they still exist).

The pub has recently been refurbished and is now part of the Sizzling Pub chain. It caters for the local area with many of the other pubs in the Darnall/Handsworth area having closed down. It was awarded a cask marque in 2015. It serves food and has a big screen for sports and, like other such chains, promotes itself to the family market with a range of good value food.

Chapter Three

Woodhouse to Gleadless Townend

The Angel, Woodhouse

Originally situated on Chapel Street at Woodhouse, the Angel Inn moved to its present site in the 1920s when the original pub was demolished because of road widening. In the early nineteenth century, the inn was called the Bull; the name was changed to the Angel sometime between 1851 and 1863 when the landlord was James Littlewood. William and Elizabeth Staniforth took over until the 1880s when the licence was transferred to the Mallinder family. Harry Pashley, the son-in-law of the Mallinders, was the last landlord of the old pub. He didn't take on the licence when it transferred to the new premises in what was Prospect House on Sheffield Road. This house was on the outskirts of the centre of Woodhouse village, close to Woodhouse West End and overlooking the nearby coal mining industry and sewage works of the Shire Brook valley.

The first landlord of the pub in its new premises was Ernest Dyson, a former butcher in Woodhouse. Prospect House was built as a large private dwelling and early photographs show extensive gardens and outbuildings. The exterior of the central building is still

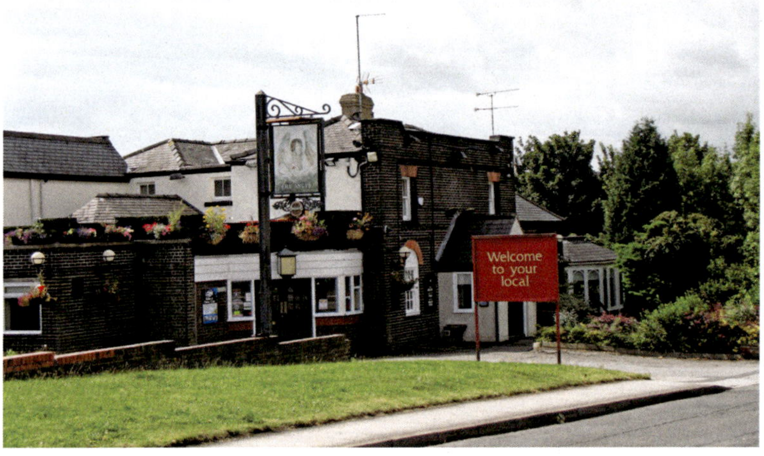

The Angel, from Sheffield Road, showing the complex of buildings.

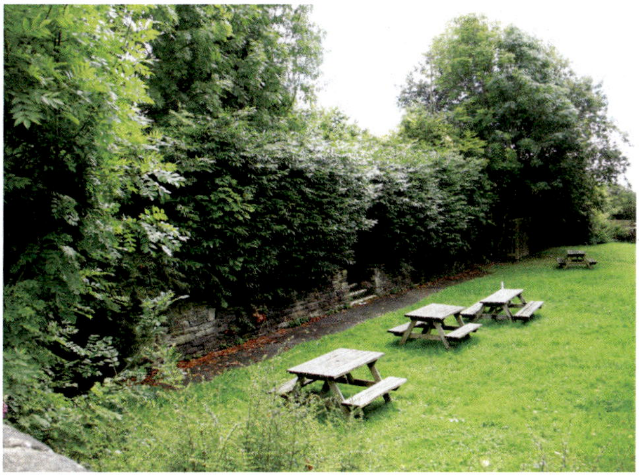

The Angel pub garden.

recognisable as the old house but there is now a conservatory on the right-hand side of the building which overlooks gardens and an outside seating area. The inn was first owned by the Hope and Anchor brewery and, by the mid-1960s, it was a Tetley's pub. It then transferred to the Stones brewery. Now part of the Trust Inns group, it has recently attracted mixed reviews from local websites. The sign depicting the Angel is modern; previously it appears that the sign was used to advertise the brewery.

The Cross Keys, Handsworth

Next to the historic parish church of St Mary's at Handsworth, The Cross Keys is a building with oak beams and small rooms showing its ancient origins. It is a popular pub. The premises had a major refit in 1991. To boost trade the then landlords, Terry and Judy Spalding, tried a very novel way to market the place. They released 600 balloons into the air. Each one contained a message from the pub and a voucher for a free drink. The ruse presumably did some good as the pub is still there and

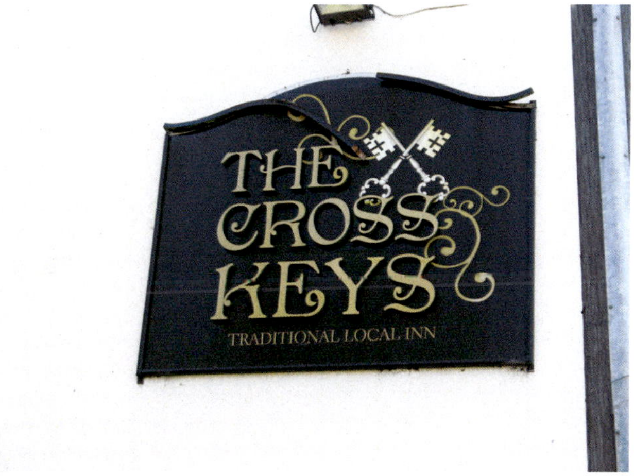

The Cross Keys sign on the side of the building.

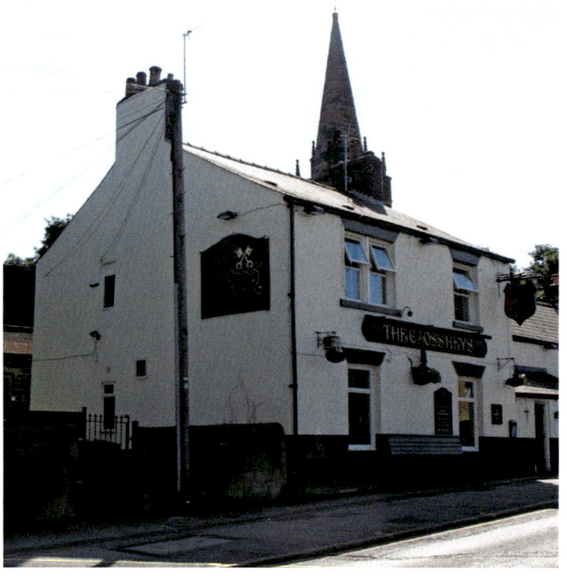

The Cross Keys with St Mary's Church spire in the background.

popular. Sadly the cask-conditioned Stones bitter, for which it was famed, has survived less well! An old building, there are rumours and secrets associated with the Cross Keys down the years. It is believed by some that there is a secret tunnel linking the pub with the Manor Lodge over a mile distant. Geology and topography suggest this is not possible, but it is a nice myth. More plausible is the idea that there was a tunnel used to link the building with another old hall nearby. Others suggest that there are also ghostly happenings with one landlord in the 1980s, admitting that although he had never seen or felt anything his dog bristled and stared at one corner of an upstairs room. Recent landlords include Frank Francis-Taylor (retired 1990), who married Connie, the widow of the previous landlord. The father of the latter, Joe Francis, had been licensee since about 1930.

This public house has the distinction of being one of the few in the UK whose buildings were originally within a churchyard and its back door still leads straight onto the church's graveyard. The first building on the site of the pub was built at the side of the churchyard in the mid-thirteenth century to house the chaplains and lay clerks for St Mary's, the parish church. It continued as the Church House until the mid-sixteenth century when it became a school. It was sold to the parish clerk, Joseph Smith, in 1800 and in 1804 the building was granted an ale licence. By the 1820s it had been named The Cross Keys, a name with a religious background, associated with St Peter as the keeper of the keys of Heaven. Its association with the churchyard and religion has given rise to several stories about secret tunnels and ghostly apparitions. The pub has been extended over the years and modernised, although it is still possible to see the outline of the oldest building in the centre of the current buildings. It is a popular local pub and fulfils a traditional role by hosting the Handsworth Sword Dancers when they dance outside the churchyard on Boxing Day.

The Sword Dancer, Handsworth

This is a new pub, opened in 2012, and is another in the Hungry Horse chain, which promotes itself as a family-oriented pub with value meals and nightly deals, promotions and quizzes. There are several rooms, including a conservatory and outside eating areas, which are pleasant to sit in on summer evenings even though it is close to a main road. It is the only pub of this name in the country and is named after the local Handsworth Sword Dancing Team, which has been in existence for over a hundred years. It is said that at some unknown time in the past, a sword dance for eight men was developed at Handsworth. This is still performed today to the traditional pattern where the dancers wear dragoon-type uniforms and carry longswords of inflexible steel about 1 metre in length. Shortly after the beginning of the ten-minute dance, they join to form a complete ring and perform a series of complex 'figures', ending with a 'lock' of enmeshed swords that can be carried aloft by one man. Traditionally, performances take place at Christmas in the Handsworth area and at functions and events by invitation at other places throughout the year. The dance is noted as one of the best and most inspiring of the dances that still survive in Yorkshire.

The pub has some memorabilia and a mural linked to the sword-dancing team and to the local industries of coal mining and steel making. Members of the sword-dancing

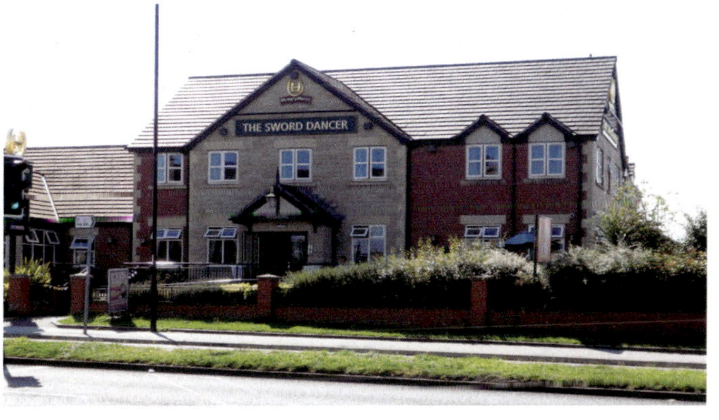

The Sword Dancer from Handsworth Road

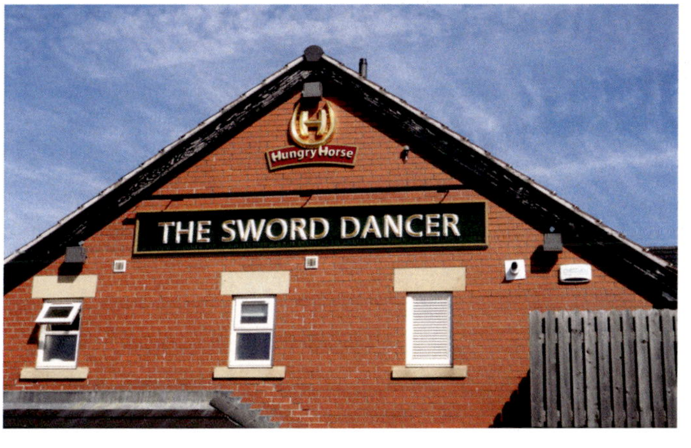

The Sword Dancer sign.

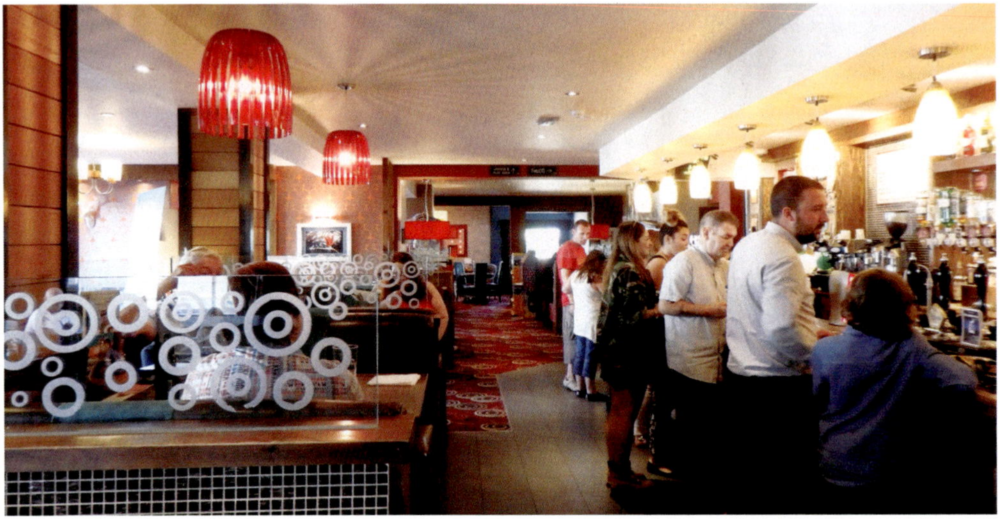

The Sword Dancer bar.

team were often drawn from these industries, especially coal mining, and it is believed that the practice of longsword dancing first started in the Durham coalfield area. As coal mining was a reserve occupation in both the First and Second World Wars, the sword-dancing team was able to continue throughout the last century. It is well worth a visit to find out more. The pub building is in part of an industrial estate that was developed in the 1950s and 1960s, on what was formerly the headquarters of the Fisher Son and Sibray Market Garden and Nurseries.

The pub chain ran a competition while the pub was being built. One of the other suggestions was the Gardeners Arms and another was the Benjamin Huntsman, as the site of Huntsman's cottage is almost opposite the pub. However, this is already the name used for a modern chain pub on Cambridge Street in the city centre. (Huntsman was the pioneer of 'cast' or 'crucible' steel manufacture and moved to Handsworth in Sheffield from Doncaster in 1740). Another suggested name was the Pickard Arms after a local war hero. The Sword Dancer was chosen as a unique name and to link the traditional dance with the local industrial past.

The Gypsy Queen, Beighton

This relatively new hostelry is one of the Hungry Horse chain of family public houses. It was purpose built in the late 1990s as part of the development of the Drakehouse area of Beighton, and refurbished in 2014. It is a large pub with several rooms and outside eating areas. Its frontage overlooks one of the entrances to the Crystal Peaks Shopping Centre and there is an extensive car park at the rear accessed off Drakehouse Lane. Its unusual name commemorates a local woman, Lucretia Smith, known as the Queen of the Gypsies, who lived in a small cottage near the church in the nineteenth century. She was famous in the local area and is buried in the parish churchyard. The pub does basic but very low-cost food and in large quantities – hence the name of the chain!

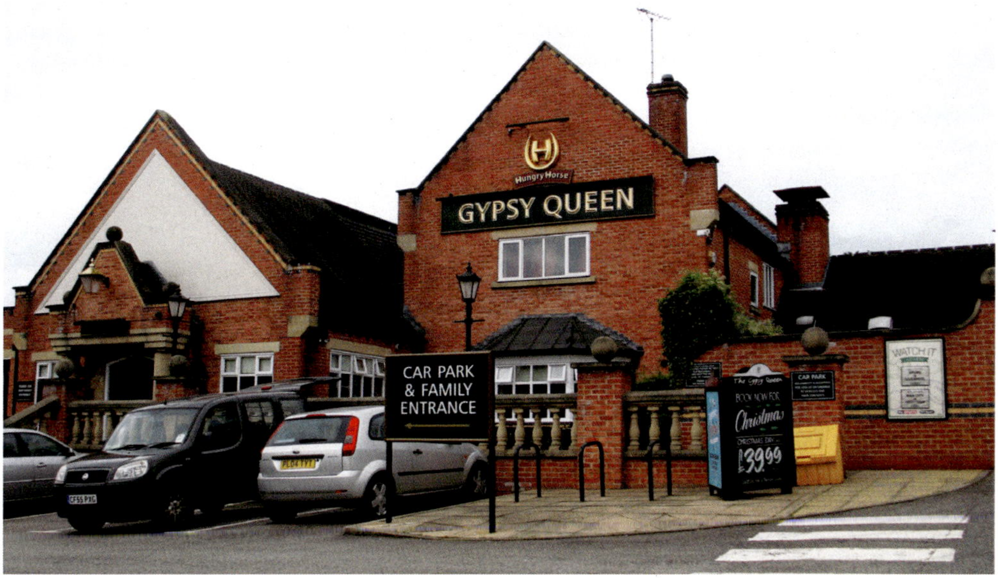

Gypsy Queen: the entrance from the car park.

The Red Lion, Gleadless Townend

The pub name 'The Red Lion' is one of the most common in the country and there are two of that name in this book. The name refers back to the tradition of using heraldic signs to publicise the existence of a place selling ale and food. The lion is a common heraldic device that was on many people's coats of arms. More famously it perhaps signifies either a supporter of John of Gaunt, founder of the Royal House of Lancaster, or represents the Scottish royal arms. This pub was built at Gleadless Townend on the edge of the old parish of Handsworth-Woodhouse. At the time it was a rural location surrounded by farms. It is unusual because the source of three streams (the Moss Brook, the Shire Brook and the Meers Brook) lies beneath the cellar of the pub. Until 1967 the two rivers or streams, the Moss Brook and the Shire Brook, formed the historic boundary between Yorkshire and Derbyshire. The pub had two main bars, which were on either side of the boundary, and when the licensing was different between the counties. Tradition has it that drinkers used to move from one bar to the other to take advantage of an extra half hour of drinking time. By the 1960s, drinkers moved down the road to the Old Harrow pub, which was still in Derbyshire, while the Red Lion was within Sheffield and South Yorkshire. Tradition also claims that the notorious burglar, Charlie Peace, drank at the pub.

Today The Red Lion is on the corner of White Lane next to shops and restaurants with the Supertram route passing by on both sides, and many patrons sit outside to watch the world go by. It is a popular, traditional local pub still with its two main bars, a taproom and a lounge. The pub organises a range of activities through the week and, according to its publicity, also welcomes groups on their way to the local Italian restaurant.

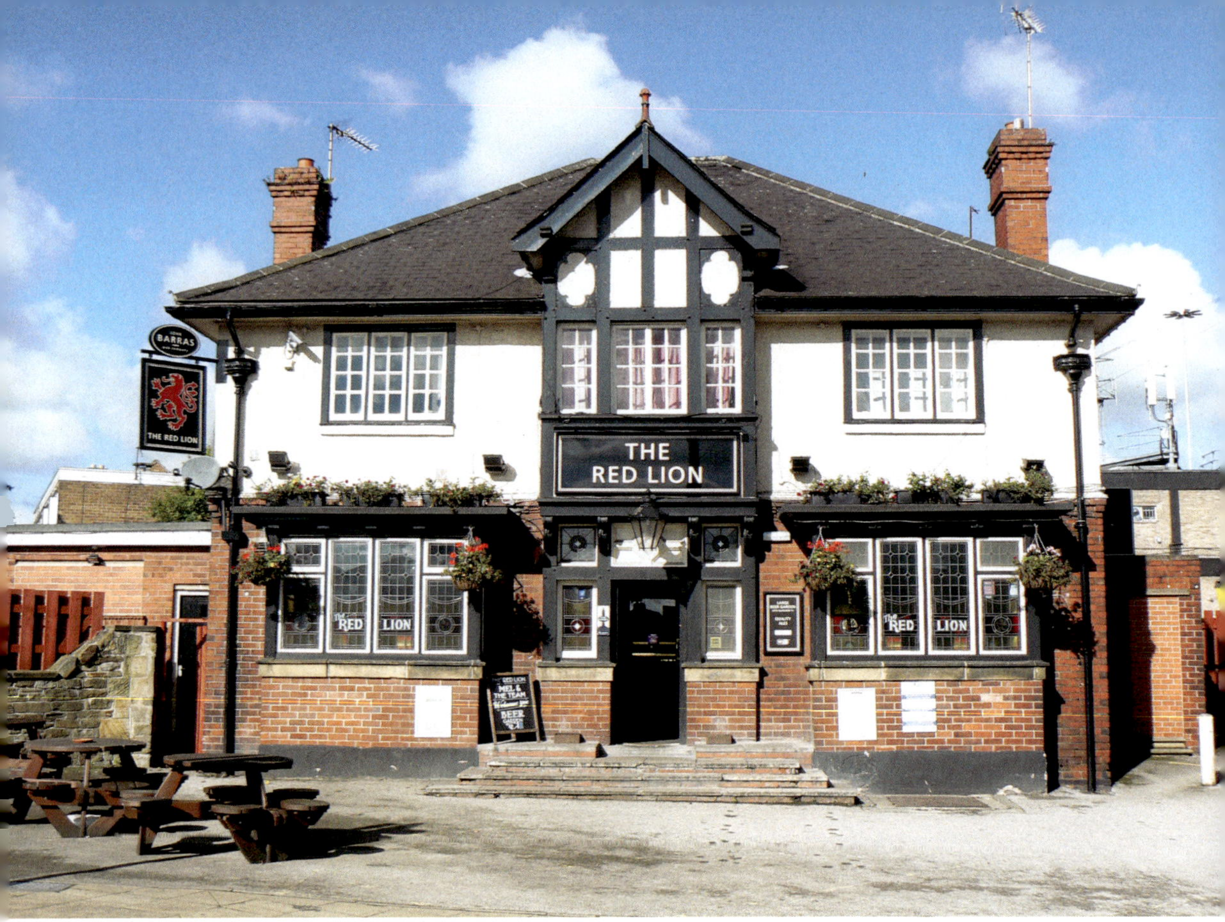

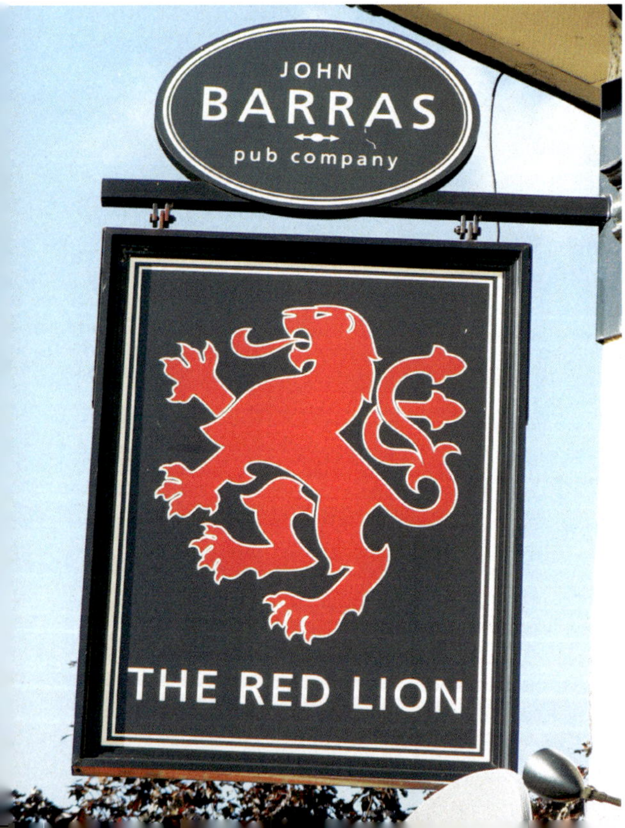

Above: The Red Lion at Gleadless Townend.

Left: The Red Lion pub sign.

Chapter Four

Norton to Nether Edge, Ecclesall, Totley and Beyond

The Bagshawe Arms

The Bagshawe Arms is one of Sheffield's oldest public houses. It was formally a rather fine country inn on the edge of Derbyshire with its name reflecting the local landowners at nearby Oakes Park. Norton village lies close by and until relatively recent times the whole area was in rural Derbyshire, and the owners of Oakes Park and the Oakes were the Bagshawe Family. This was one of the oldest and most influential families in Derbyshire, being involved in civic affairs, military matters and in the clergy. They were landowners, farmers, coal miners, and iron manufacturers of great importance to the area.

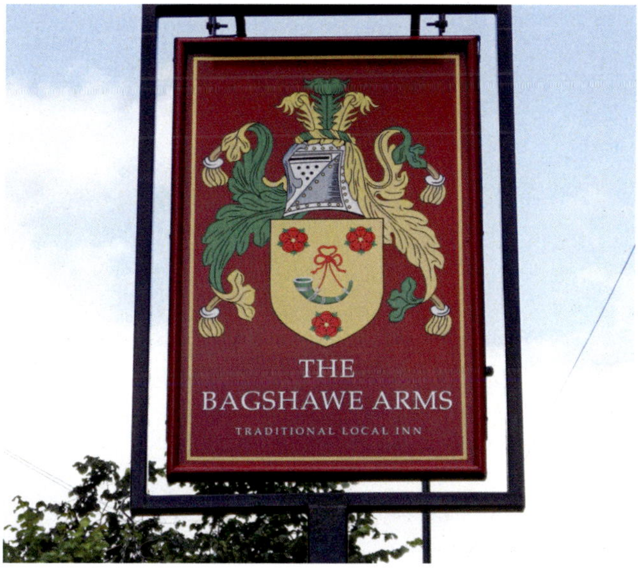

The Bagshawe Arms sign.

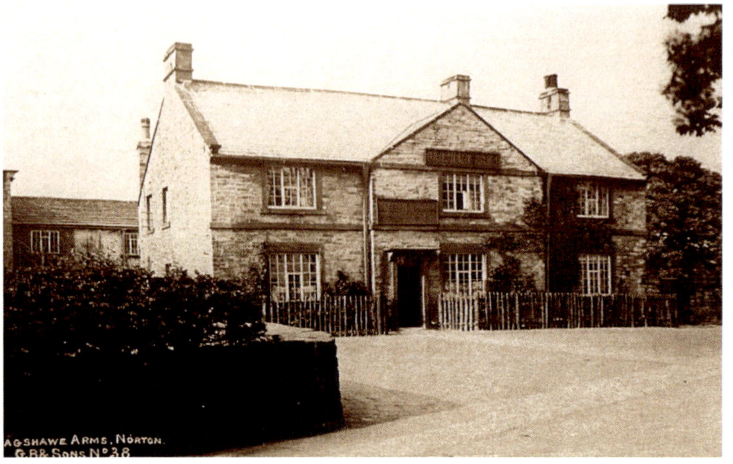

The Bagshawe Arms, Norton, in the early 1900s.

Indeed, the building was originally a farmhouse on the Bagshawe estate and an old barn still stands close by. Construction was from the local Mawfa Lane quarries; it was enlarged and renovated in 1829, serving as an inn since at least 1844. There is a stone embedded in the south end of the gable with the initials 'F. W. B.' (Francis Westby Bagshawe) and the date 1859. One of the outbuildings, with a first floor reached by an external staircase, was also used in Victorian times as the local petty sessions court. With a limited history of significant events, the visit by local writer and poet, John Thomas, seems to be a highlight when he later wrote of the fine pig's chap, eggs and beer that he had consumed!

In the early nineteenth century, one owner or landlord was a very industrious man named George Rogers. He was not only the landlord, but a printer by trade, and also worked for the *Weekly Independent* in addition to being a working farmer and secretary of the Farmers' Club. He was named by the locals 'Lord George' – possibly because of his energetic, non-stop, affluent lifestyle.

Like many old public houses, The Bagshawe Arms has its claim to hauntings! On 26–27 November 2011, using night vision video with infrared lighting, a 'paranormal investigation' took place in the Old Court House and the main bar. You can view the results on YouTube.

The building is listed but Douglas Lamb still considered it to have been 'modernised and spoilt'. For many years it was a Yates's Wine Lodge. It is still a popular drinking establishment for the nearby Gleadless estate.

The Nailmakers, Norton

Built in 1627, this remarkable building on Backmoor Road is in fact one of the oldest pubs in South Yorkshire and its name reflects the local industry in nail making. It was still a traditional 'no-frills' pub in the 1960s when the grandfather of one of the authors used to visit to meet his friends, and have a game of dominoes and cribbage. The landlord took no nonsense and on one occasion was about to challenge a group of young men as to their ages when the author's grandfather recognised his grandson,

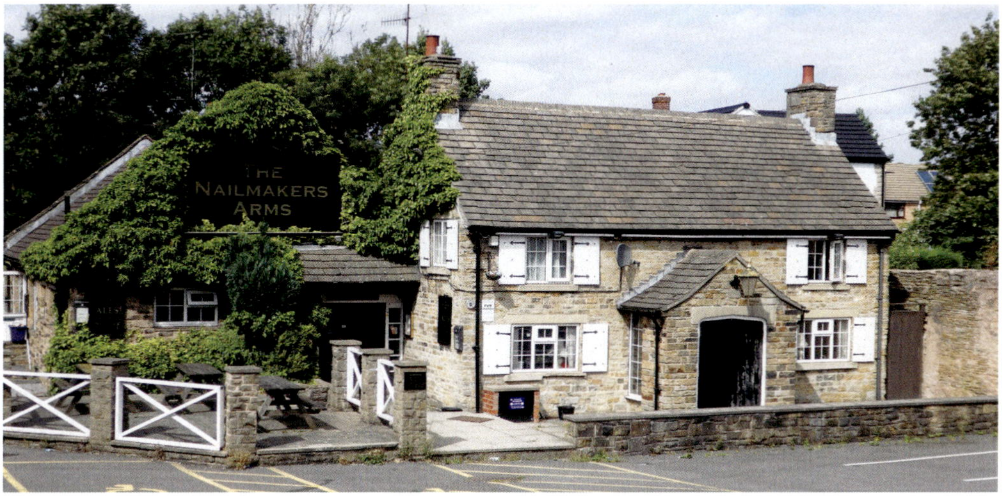

Above: The Nailmakers Arms public house.

Right: The Nailmakers Arms public house sign.

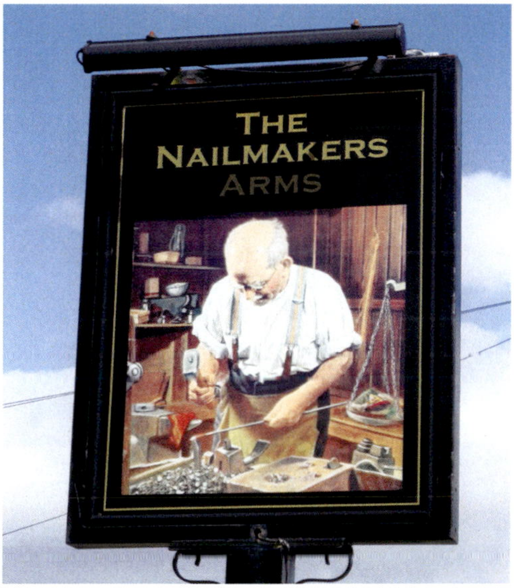

said hello, and the group was allowed in. It then became a favourite of not only the grandfather but also the grandson. Sadly the pub has suffered many decades of tasteless and inappropriate 'modernisation' and refurbishment; in the 1970s it was renowned as a popular place for heavy drinking and a disco. The ancient hostelry, though retaining its low ceilings, has never really recovered! In the old buildings behind the pub, the original landlords brewed their own beers – a common practice before modern-day commercial breweries took over.

In August 1984, The Nailmakers had a major refit costing about £50,000 for William Youngers and for the landlord at the time, Pat Williams. The reopening ceremony was attended by national nail-bending champion Ben Read from Hampshire. Aged 51 years, Ben apparently bent six-inch nails for charity and could do around one hundred every thirteen and a half minutes. He challenged customers fifty pence per nail to try and match him, though it is not clear how you go about 'bending nails'! However, the act of bending nails is something that used to be seen by the strong men on the old music hall circuit or at the circus. These men, and occasionally women, used to tear up London phone books, bend 6-inch steel nails, bend iron bars and have objects thrown at their tensed body to prove their strength. Nail bending requires great hand and wrist strength. Bending a 6-inch nail is said to be the first step to gaining the entrance into the performing strongman world.

Some dart players in England think throwing darts can get boring, so they take some 6-inch nails and use them instead. Joe Hitchcock used to love to beat 'the champs' in this fashion. One of his favourite tricks was to 'nail' a button from between someone's outstretched fingers.

The modern pub is still welcoming and in winter has an open fire. It is described as a 'no nonsense' local estate pub serving beer but not food; there is a pool room, darts, plus traditional games, and a sizeable function room.

The Sportsman, Harvey Clough Road and Warminster Road

This is a very traditional locals' pub on the main bus route from Meersbrook to Norton, which by the early 2000s had seen better days. However, a major refurbishment around 2007 and 2008 has given the pub a new lease of life and it is now a thriving community pub. Along with beers and other drinks, The Sportsman also now offers food. The pub started life in the nineteenth century as the area around Heeley and Meersbrook developed. At that time it had a bowling green next to it and is perhaps where the name of the pub originates. The Sportsman was a popular name for a pub in the

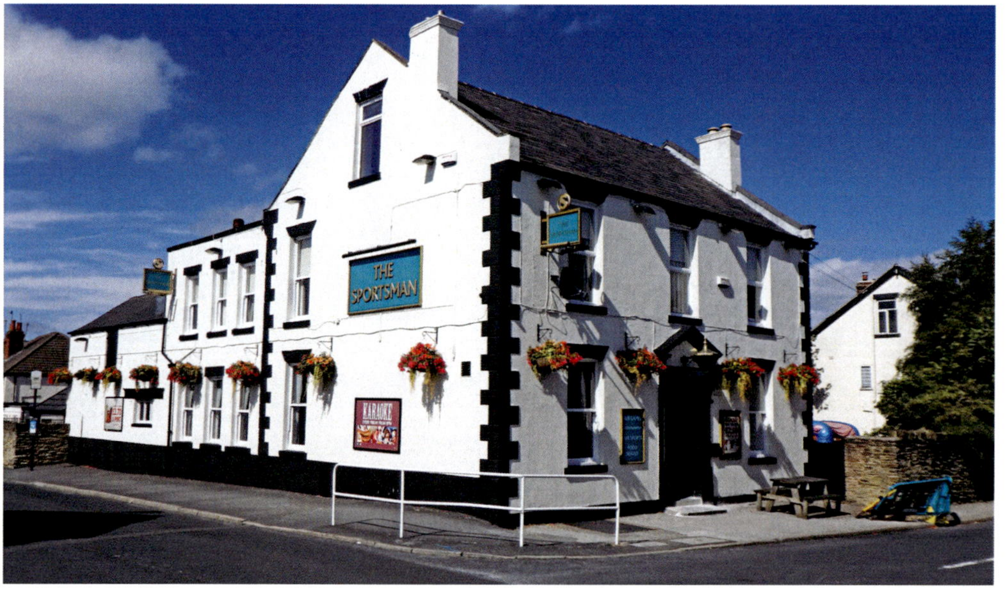

The Sportsman on Harvey Clough Road.

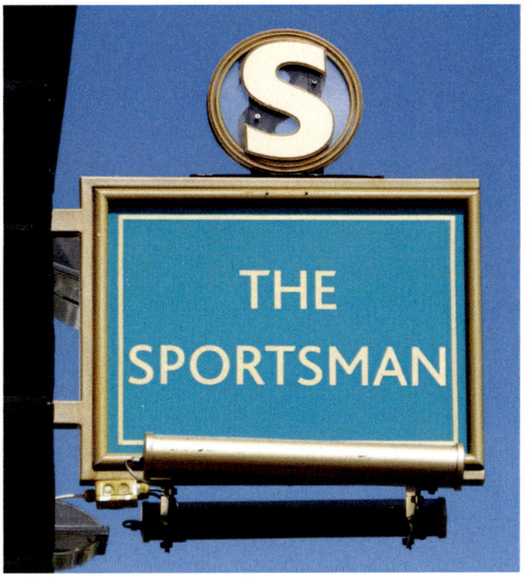

The Sportsman pub sign.

Sheffield area and there were several with associations with sports grounds providing refreshments for players and supporters. An old sign over the side door shows that one of the landlords was named Albert Potts. He was licensed as a 'purveyor of ales, beers, porter, wine, spirits and tobacco both on and off the premises.' In common with many other pubs, the landlord also operated an 'off-licence' where people could buy alcohol and tobacco for home consumption. By the 1960s, in common with many other pubs in Sheffield, the pub had been taken over by Tetley's.

The Big Tree, Chesterfield Road, Woodseats

Until 1935 the Big Tree was called the Mason's Arms. However, in a remarkable turn of events, a circus elephant tethered to the tree outside the pub managed to rip off a major branch and the tree subsequently died. When the original tree was replaced,

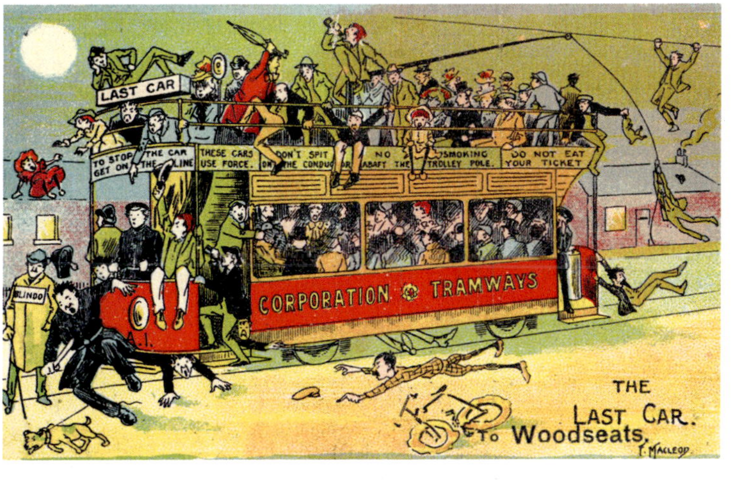

The Last Car to Woodseats, 1907, by the Big Tree.

the pub was renamed, though the new tree was felled because of disease in November 1985, and the present tree is the third in line. At this time the pub was run by Miss Yorkshire Television, Jill Saxby, and her fiancé Peter Yates.

It is suggested that the preacher from Epworth and founder of the Methodist Church, Revd John Wesley, preached under the shelter of the original great tree as he gave a sermon to the local villagers in Woodseats. Another unique claim to fame is that the renowned sculptor (later Sir) Francis Chantrey is said to have sat in the shade of the tree as he produced his earlier wood carvings. Originally built around 1825 or earlier, the present building is relatively new, being reconstructed around 1901. It still has floor tiles under the carpets that show the mason's trade and there are mason's signs on the gable ends that face the road. By the 1970s, this hostelry had something of a reputation for under-age drinking and a somewhat threatening clientele from a nearby estate. It was not unknown for groups of well-oiled youths to rampage down to places like Millhouses to seek out confrontation with the 'posh' locals of the pubs down there. In more recent times, things have settled and are more civilised!

In 1982, the Big Tree became Sheffield's first 'Brewburger' – an American-style chain – having had a range of other owners such as Strouts' Brewery and Tennant Brothers. This is still a popular drinking pub for the nearby housing estates, serving low-cost, basic food. The Big Tree benefits from the hustle and bustle of the Woodseats shopping area.

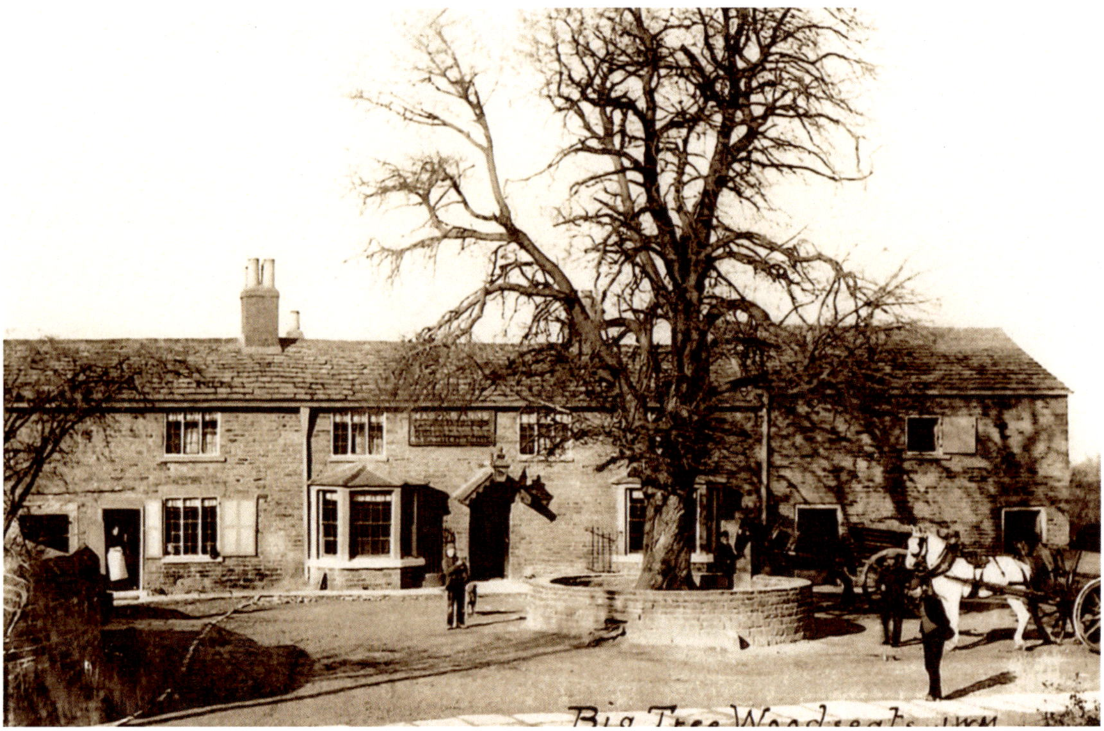

The Big Tree at Woodseats in the early 1900s.

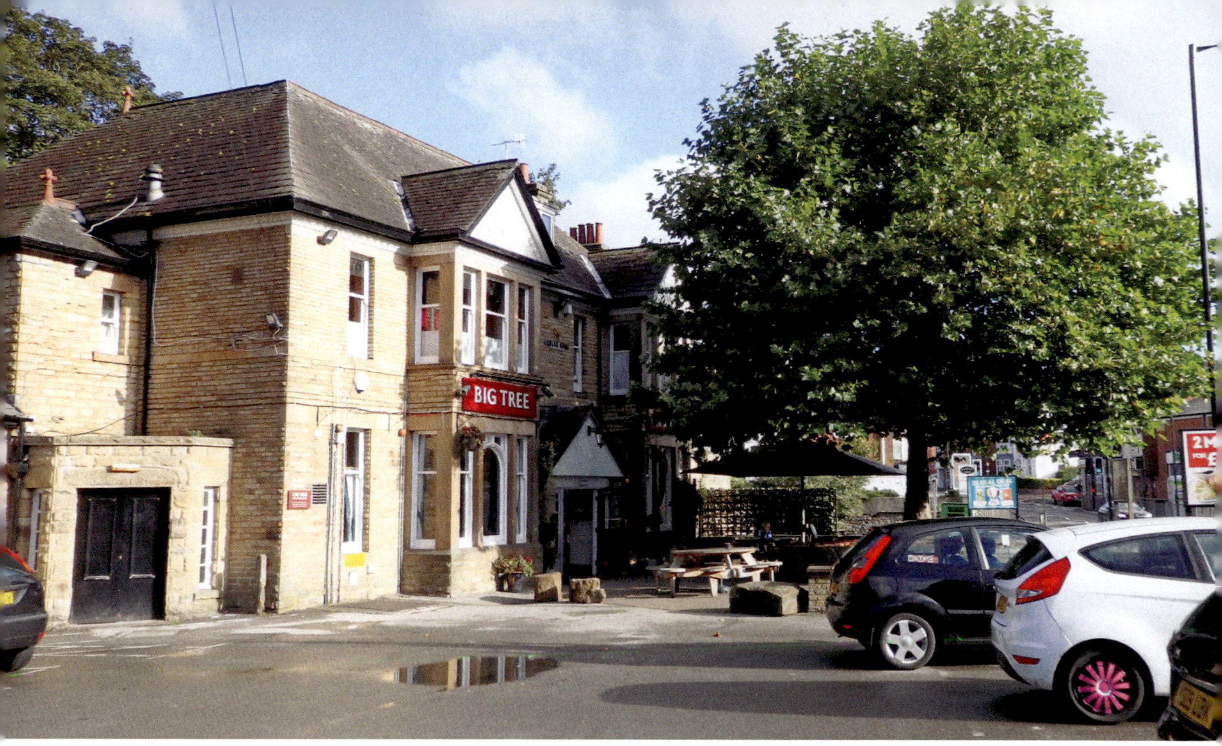

Above: The Big Tree.

Below: The Big Tree bar.

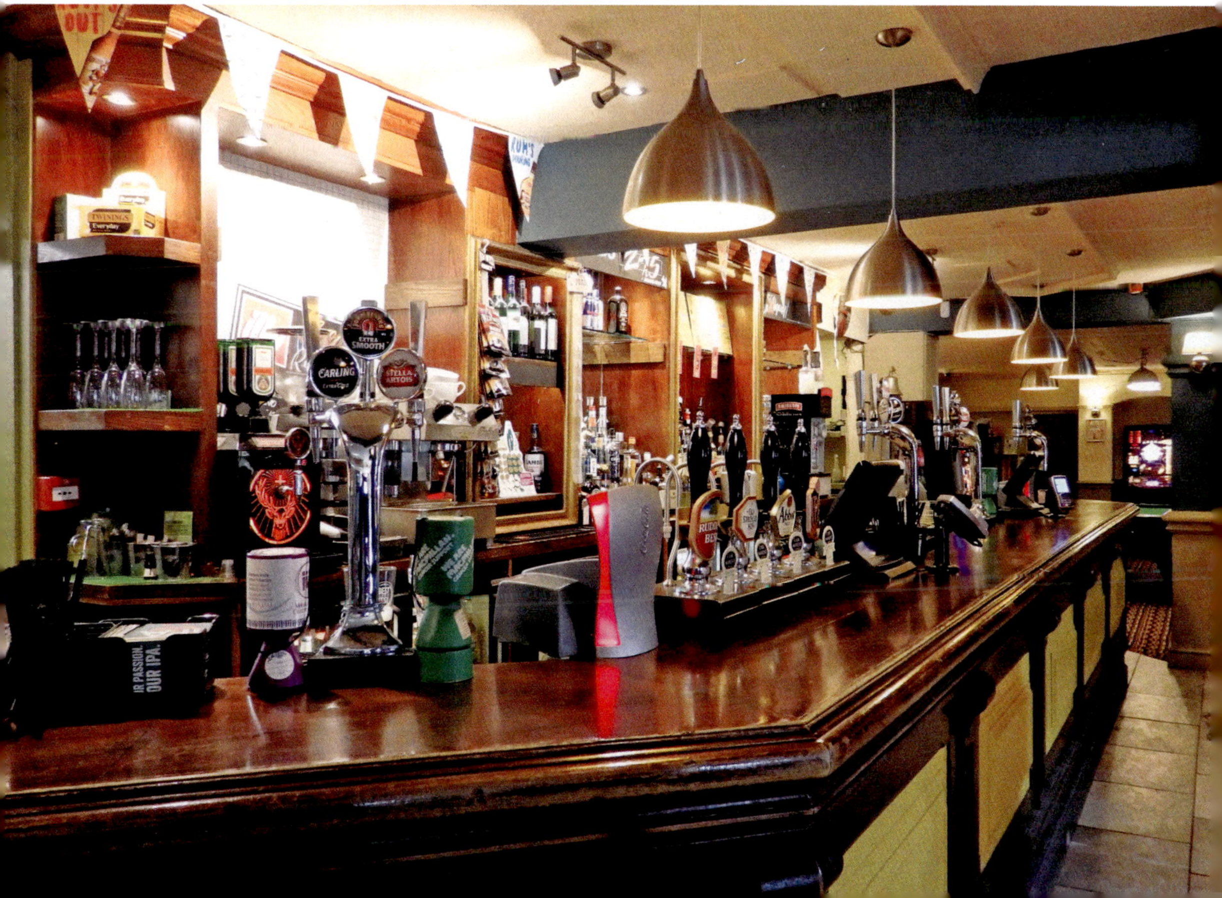

The White Lion, Chesterfield Road, Heeley

Situated on the busy Chesterfield Road out of Sheffield during the 1700s and 1800s, this location would have been close to the town and Yorkshire border with Derbyshire. The road out to the south and leading to Chesterfield, Derby and then London, was a major throughway. A public house here would be a good location to gather in passing trade, and indeed, The White Lion has been a hostelry since 1781. In 1825, Thomas Brandon was the landlord and is described in the trade directory as a licensed victualler, providing food as well as beverages. By then the Heeley area was starting to develop as one of Sheffield's main industrial areas, with terraced housing for local workers also being built. The White Lion was well placed to cater for this new community and has been doing so ever since. The pub's owners describe it as a heritage pub steeped in Sheffield history and renowned for its live music. The pub has free events all week and boasts ten cask ales and ciders, plus a good selection of malt whiskies. Above all it has a warm, friendly atmosphere – a traditional pub. The White Lion has always had a great reputation as a friendly place to drink or a good location for a free venue for meetings and activities.

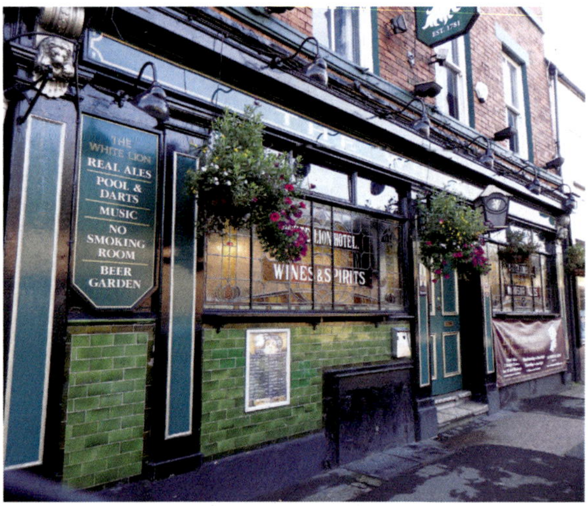

The White Lion, Heeley.

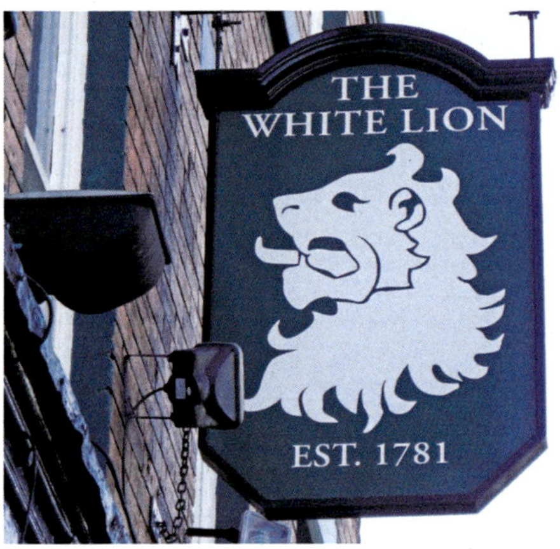

The White Lion inn sign.

The Shakespeare or Brothers, Well Road, Heeley

Ye Olde Shakespeare Inn was also known to regulars as 'The Shakey' but is now known as The Brothers Arms. In its earlier days, up to the 1950s, it was the Shakespeare Inn or Shakespeare Tavern. It dates back to the early nineteenth century when Mark Robinson was listed as the landlord. Between 1854 and 1879, the landlord was William Webster. In the 1850s, William was shown in the trade directory as being a 'pocket blade grinder' and by the 1870s as a farmer – two common occupations for the local area.

Advertisements on the front of the pub in the 1920s tell customers to 'Ask for Bass'. In 1951 the landlord was Joseph Fox. Then, having had the same landlord for forty years with the late David Fox owning the pub from 27 March 1961 until 21 August 2001, the place had a series of newcomers over the next few years. Over that long period of stability this was a haunt favoured by locals and other regulars and generally packed with customers. Following the retirement of the landlord and landlady, the pub fell on more troubled times and lost much of the earlier popularity. However, more recently it has been bought by a consortium of the local Sheffield band The Everley Pregnant Brothers, including BBC Radio Sheffield's Toby Foster and local artist, Pete McKee. Following a major refurbishment, the pub has reopened with a new name and is now thriving once again.

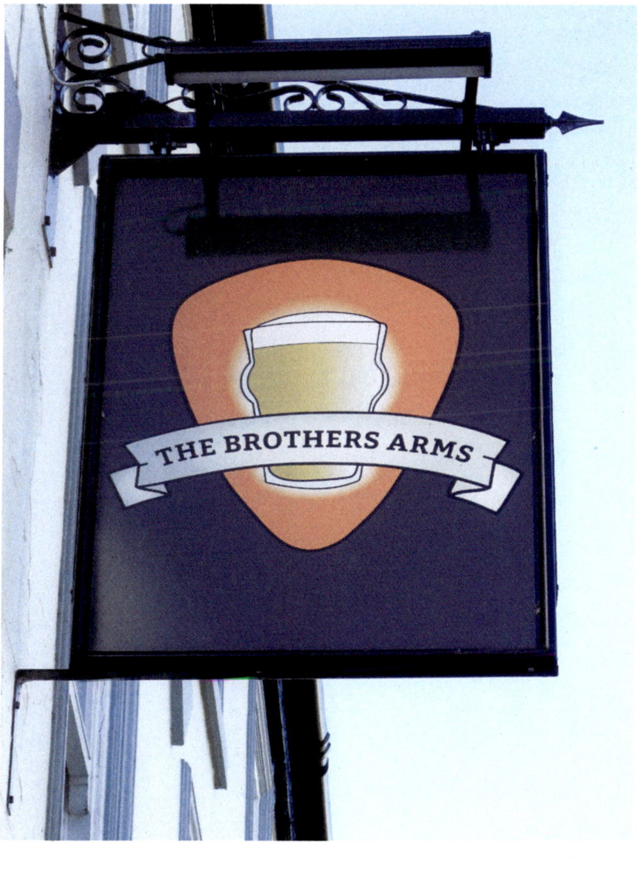

The Brothers Arms inn sign.

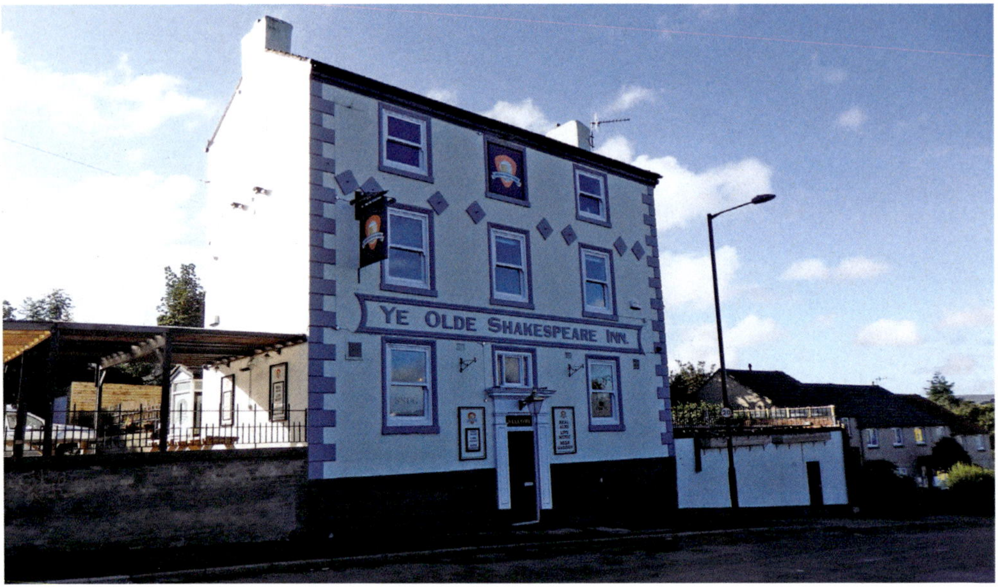

The Brothers Arms.

The Sheaf View, Gleadless Road, Heeley

One of the authors recalls, in the 1970s or early 1980s, calling in at The Sheaf View prior to the demolition of local houses and the building of the modern estate. 'It really was like walking into someone's front room. A group of local folk were huddled into a small bar with several cats. The noise momentarily paused and everyone greeted us and we were made welcome'. So this is another fine old Sheffield pub with a long pedigree and is sat in a landscape that has changed dramatically over the last few decades; a remarkable connection to a largely forgotten past. The old building remains and is unspoilt but has had a modest extension and a beer garden added.

It still has an excellent reputation for being cosy and very friendly. 'Real beer and no music, this pub is easily the best place in Sheffield to enjoy a pint of interesting beer. There is a good amount of space and seats, and two outdoor seating areas including one for smokers.' Another reviewer states that it is a 'cracking pub, popular with the locals, with a great range of cask ales and craft beers. No unfined cask ales were available but the barman did say they are occasionally featured. I enjoyed a very tasty can of vegan friendly Moor Brewing Company 'Hoppiness' and they also had other favourites such as Flying Dog Pale Ale. We sat on the terrace and were impressed by the beautiful hanging basket flower displays and the surrounding rowan trees, laden with berries. No fruit machines, television or jukebox, child and dog friendly, I am sure this pub would meet the criteria for an Asset of Community Value.'

Essentially, this small pub is part of a group of similar hostelries operating a micro-brewery called Neepsend Brewery, so their own beers feature alongside other local favourites. They are well priced and tasty, and The Sheaf is a lovely pub where 'you can meet like-minded folk to enjoy good ale'. You can't say fairer than that.

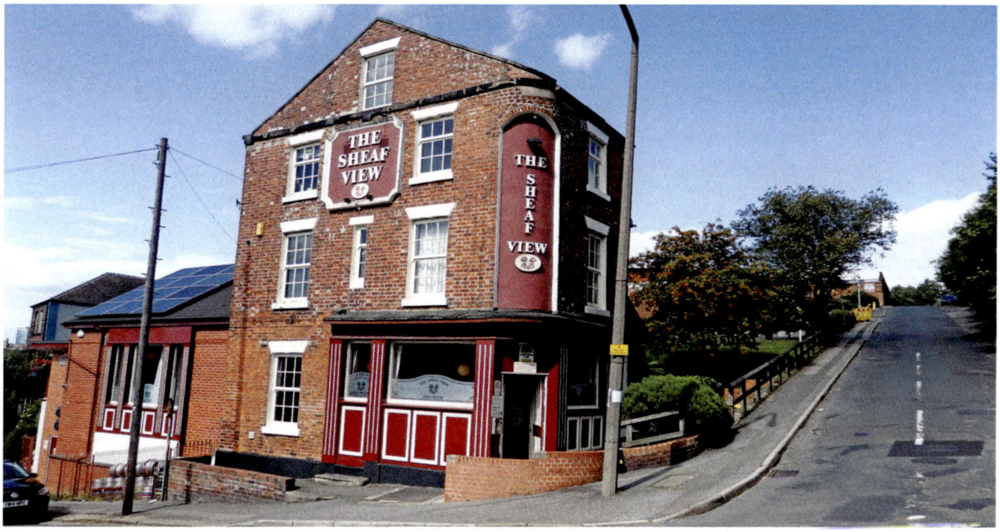

Above: The Sheaf View.

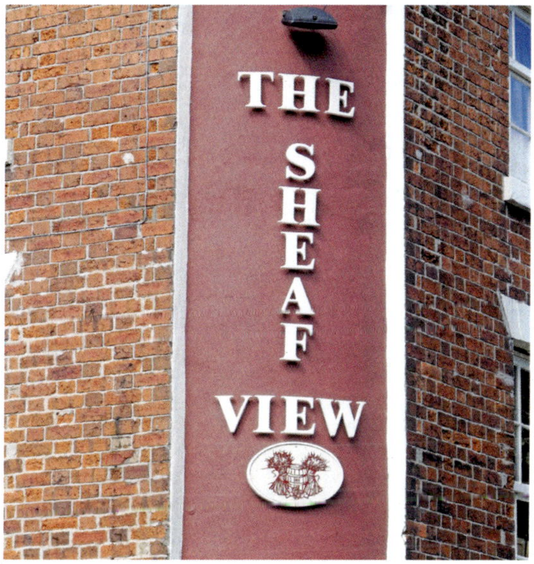

Right: The corner Sheaf View sign.

The Broadfield, Abbeydale Road

Today, this is described as a bright, rustic-styled Victorian pub with mismatched tables, wood burner and stripped floors, and now serving good food as well as drink. The Broadfield was built in the 1890s by Albert Twigg. The walls of the present-day pub are full of memorabilia from that time. It is situated on Abbeydale Road in the core of the Sheffield Antiques Quarter. When it was first opened the Broadfield would have been on the edge of countryside and green fields, soon to be lost under Sheffield's urban sprawl. The place has a long history, with ups and downs over the years, and at times a reputation for heavy drinking and not much else. Today, following a major refit and refurbishment in 2012, the Broadfield has reinvented itself at the heart of its new

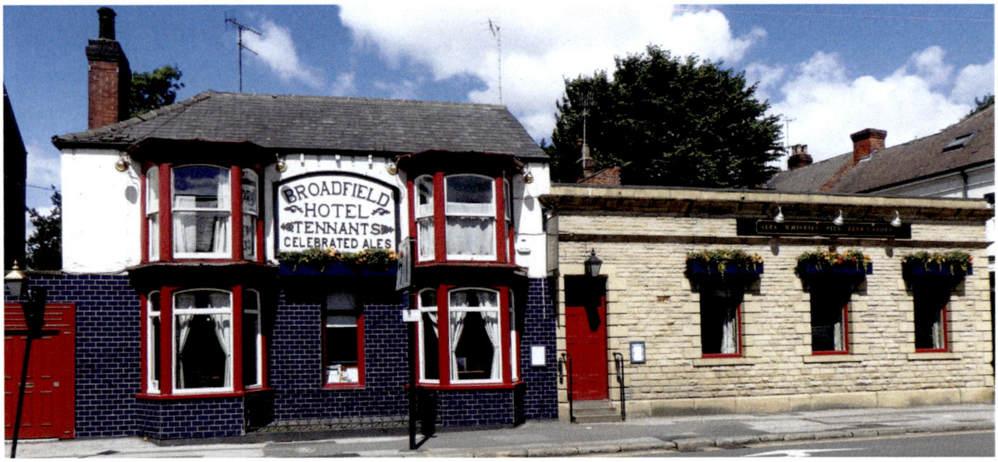

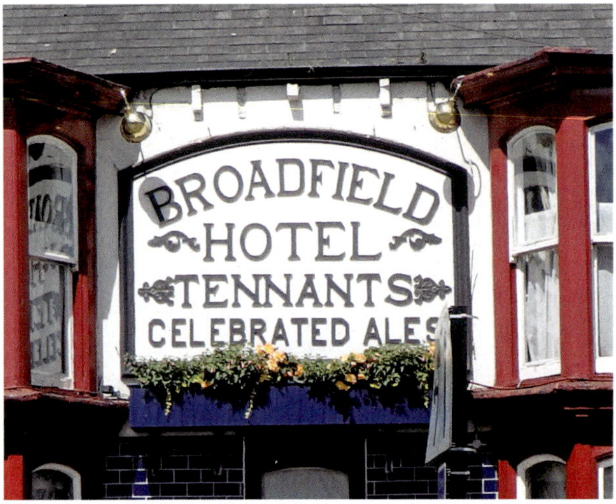

Above: The Broadfield Hotel.

Left: The Broadfield Hotel frontage and sign.

community and reflected its glory days in the late nineteenth century. There is good food and drink in a friendly atmosphere, with beers sourced from around the world, but especially from local breweries including their own. There are also good wines and spirits with, it is claimed, a single malt whisky from every working distillery in Scotland and gins including True North Sheffield dry gin.

There is always a friendly face at the bar and to bring you food to your table in the restaurant, thus ensuring your visit to the Broadfield Hotel is a happy one. Again, this is a venue that has changed and adapted to new times and new customers.

The Cross Scythes, Baslow Road, Totley

This pub was originally opened by local farmer and scythe-maker Samuel Hopkinson, hence its name. Hopkinson rented the buildings, reckoned to be around 300 years old, from local man George Greaves. The intention was clearly to capitalise on the recently opened toll road or turnpike from Sheffield, up the hill to Owler Bar (where the toll

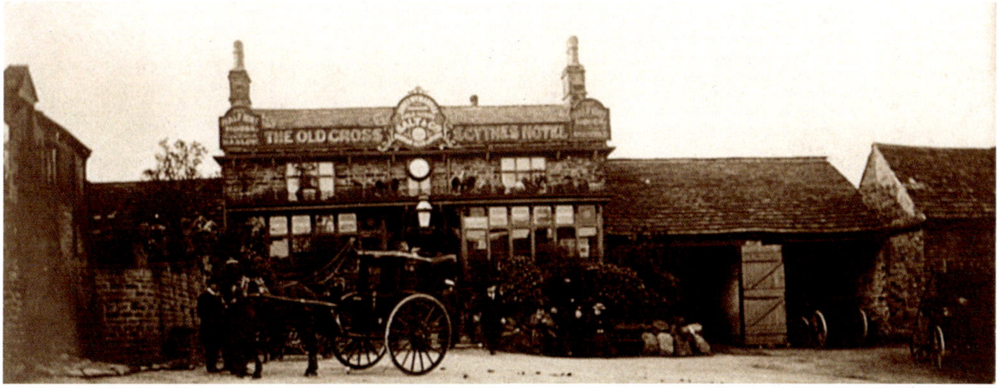

Above: The Cross Scythes at Totley, Sheffield, in the early 1900s.

Below: The Cross Scythes at Totley.

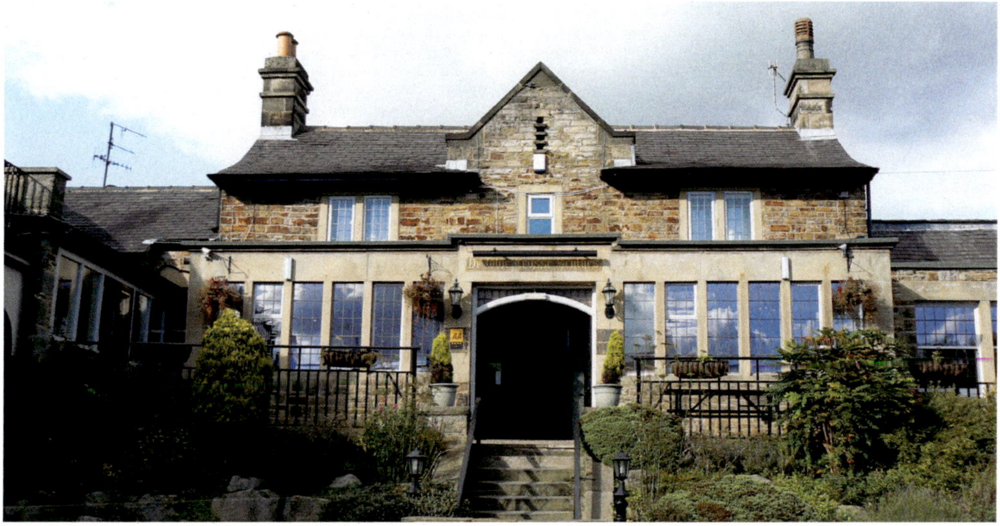

booth cottage still stands) and beyond. The pub stands a little way back from the road with the modern car park at the front on the old courtyard. Subsequent landlords included Thomas Fisher, around 1836; followed by John Thorpe in 1846, when the name was changed to Ye Old Cross Scythes; John Wagstaff; Job Green until 1868; and then Thomas Brown in 1872. By 1885 a Grimesthorpe haulage business owned by Michael Cottam started a bus service to run between the Cross Scythes and the newly-opened Dore and Totley Railway Station at the bottom of Totley Rise. The courtyard of the pub was for many years the terminus of the regular Totley bus services, the No. 24 from town. There is still a bus stop outside the pub car park although it is no longer the terminus for the route. Rather controversially, that was moved another half mile out into the countryside to a purpose-built returning circle, though after local protests the excessive lighting was reduced.

In recent years, the pub has been thoroughly refurbished and now offers upmarket food and accommodation to tap into the burgeoning tourism market of the nearby Peak District National Park.

The Cricket Inn, Penny Lane, Totley

The Cricket Inn is set snugly in the Totley Bents on the south-western edge of Sheffield and the Peak District. It is a little off the beaten track, but turn right off Baslow Road onto Hillfoot Road and continue to follow the hill down into the valley. Turning left just after another great pub, the Crown Inn, you are on Penny Lane. The Cricket Inn is located on the left just before the playing fields. This is an exceptional location, even if somewhat hard to find. When you get there it has incredible warmth and a unique character. The food is suggested by the proprietors to be something that everyone will really enjoy based on generous portions, local and seasonal ingredients and totally traceable products from brilliant suppliers.

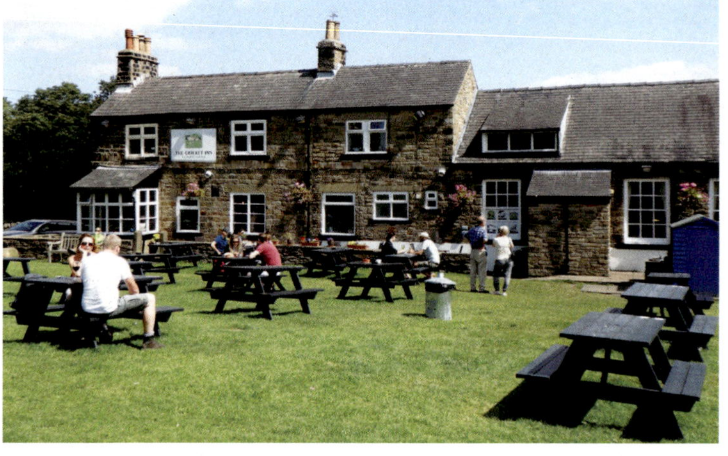

The Cricket Inn with drinkers outside enjoying the summer.

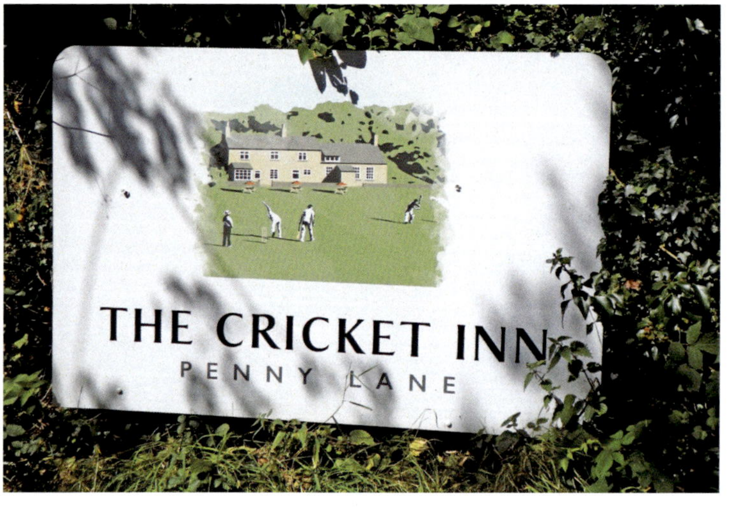

The Cricket Inn sign.

This is a pub with a long tradition of good food and good hospitality. In the winter you can watch football being played on the nearby pitch and in the summer you really get the feel of the English village atmosphere when the local cricket team take on their opponents. Situated in the shadow of the once-important 'Totley Bole' lead smelting site and overshadowed by the purple moors, it has also had its ups and downs over the years with some interesting and colourful landlords. Today however, The Cricket Inn is one of a number of houses now run on behalf of Thornbridge Brewery at Bakewell. The premises began life as a farmhouse owned by a Mr W. Green in 1865. At the time the building was right on the edge of Totley village, as it still is. Close by and to the west lie the extensive moors and bogs of the Dark Peak. Like many pubs this was formerly a farmhouse and in the case of the Cricket, it was first licensed to sell alcohol in 1889 when the owner of the farmhouse, John Aston, opened the premises as The Cricket Inn. The incentive was the influx of Irish navvies working on the nearby railway tunnel.

During the latter part of the nineteenth century, the area was dominated by the massive construction work for the Totley Tunnel, part of a major project to link Sheffield and Manchester by railway. The tunnel was finally completed in 1893 but it had not been easy and was an amazing feat of engineering and human muscle-power by the navvies. A big problem was the water held in the geological aquifers of the area, with one newspaper stating that the tunnel workers had 'the miraculous power of Moses, for whenever a rock was struck, water sprang out of it'; at least 26,000 gallons per hour had to be pumped away as work progressed during 1889. Presumably the pub and its hospitality, however Spartan at the time, would have made a welcome break for workers and their families. The conditions of the tunnel itself and the temporary 'village' provided for them were pretty awful. Disease and danger were a constant presence with accidents, explosions and injuries, but also trench foot, smallpox and typhoid. At one point the casualties were so great and mortality so frequent that the old barn of the pub was used as a temporary mortuary. The men constructed the second-longest tunnel in the UK at the time, with the first passenger train passing through in 1894.

Since that time The Cricket Inn has had numerous owners, including Oscar Creswick in the 1920s and a member of the Totley tug of war team in 1919. There was also a relative of the present landlord Richard Smith – his grandfather's cousin. Richard and Thornbridge Brewery combined to give the pub a new start in 2007, the year of the Sheffield floods, so the tradition of huge amounts of water continued. The pub now offers excellent beers from local to international, and an extensive and interesting food menu. You can even get to enjoy this in a one-time mortuary.

The Norfolk Arms, Ringinglow

This is a popular tourist pub offering accommodation, conference facilities, a wedding venue and function room, combined with good food. It is situated on the edge of the Peak District National Park and has its origin as a 'turnpike' inn situated opposite the toll booth now fondly referred to as the 'Round House', which is of course not 'round' but octagonal! Built in the late 1700s to service the turnpike road from Sheffield to Chapel-en-le-Frith and Buxton, this route opened in 1758. By 1798 the Ringinglow turnpike was taking £421 per annum, presumably it was this passing trade that led to

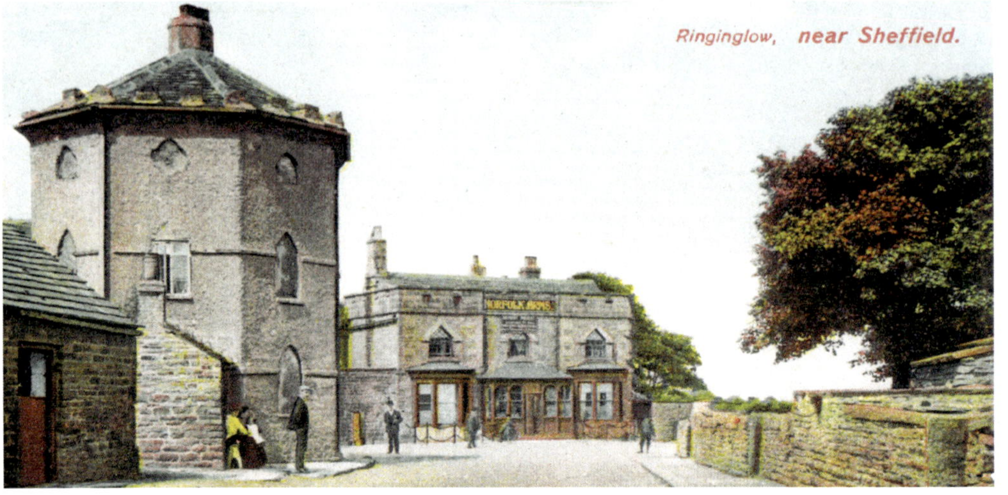

Above: The Roundhouse and Norfolk Arms at Ringinglow, Sheffield, in the early 1900s.

Below: The Norfolk Arms, Ringinglow.

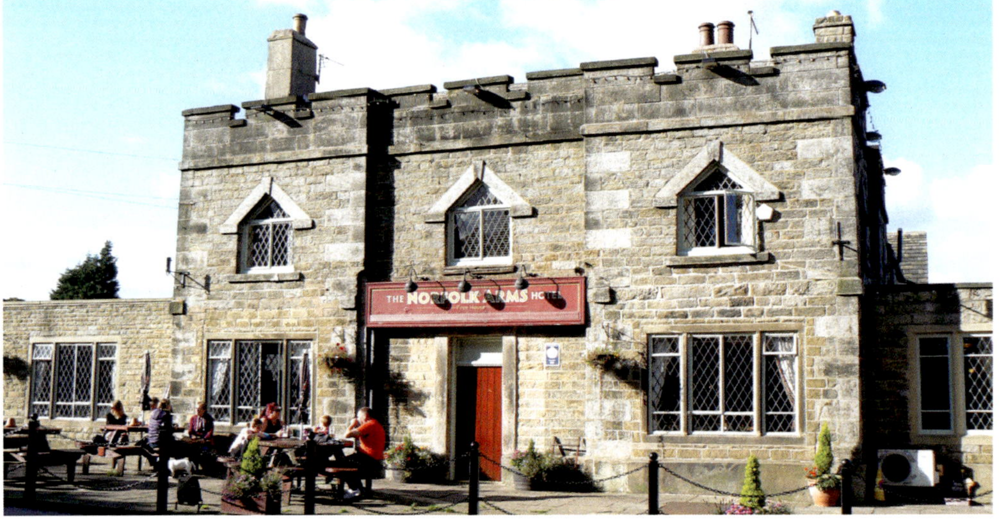

the opening in 1844 of the then Ringinglow Inn as a coach house. One early publicity stunt that boosted visitor numbers to the pub was a hoax by local journalists who ran an article entitled 'Horrible murder at Ringinglow' in 1876 and followed it with one that claimed 'Body found!' None of this was true; it was rumoured to be a prank pulled off by the then landlord, Mr Garratt. It is also suggested that the painting of the 'Laughing Cavalier' hanging on the pub wall was somehow connected to the activities of resident ghost 'Eric'. A bit far-fetched maybe, but when the pub was refurbished in the 1980s, then landlady Gill Murphy took it all very seriously, making sure The Cavalier was well positioned and was a big deal. Or was it another publicity stunt?

Recently refurbished, this is now a venue offering food and drink to Sheffielders out for the evening, with good views of Sheffield and over the Mayfield valley. The Norfolk Arms also caters for events such as weddings and other parties and offers good accommodation within easy reach of the Peak Park. Not far away there is a wonderful and evocative area of wild and remote landscape with the Burbage Valley, Ringinglow Bog and Stanage Edge.

The Rising Sun, Ecclesall

The Rising Sun on Abbey Lane began life as a small cottage altered and enlarged many times over several centuries. It was noted as a public house in the late 1700s when Sampson Brookshaw was the innkeeper. He was recorded as such in a stone memorial to a dead charcoal burner or wood collier, George Yardley, who burnt to death in his cabin in Ecclesall Woods on 11 October 1786. This was a hazard of the occupation as the charcoal man tended his burning stack throughout the day and night. The memorial was erected by Sampson Brookshaw, publican; and by David Glossop, gamekeeper; Thomas Smith, beesome maker and William Brooke, salesman. We can imagine the scene as Yardley and friends had been drinking in the Rising Sun before he went back to his wigwam cabin of wood poles and turf thatch. After several pints of the local brew, probably lighting his pipe, and even perhaps affected by fumes from the burn, he fell into a deep sleep. Maybe his pipe lit the cabin or possibly a spark from the charcoal burn was the cause; but by morning he had burnt to death. One imagines his guilt-ridden friends clubbed together to provide a lasting memorial – which incidentally is not a gravestone as it is likely that there was little left to bury.

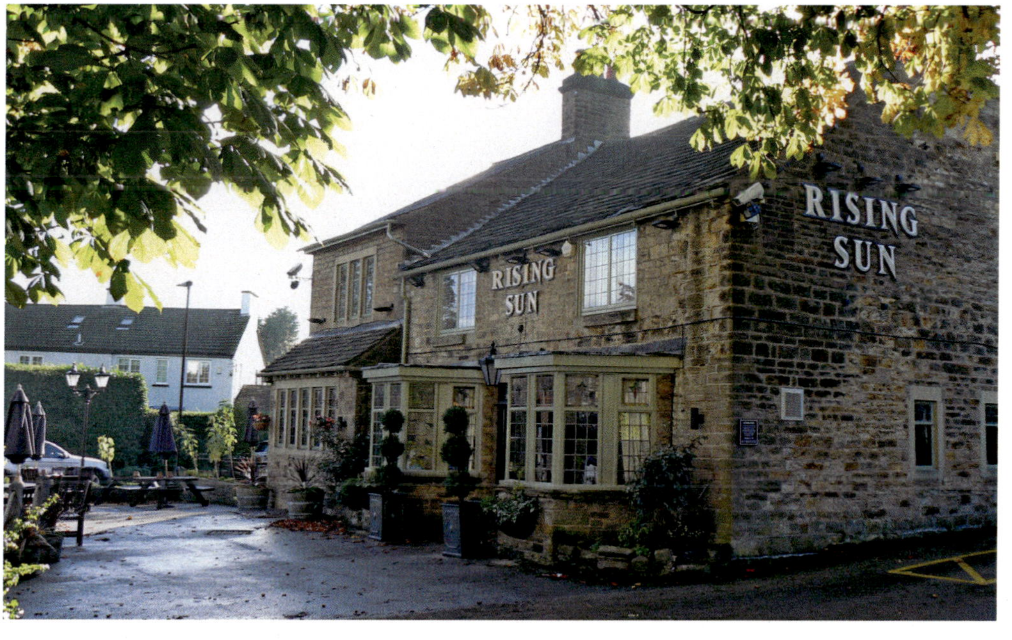

The Rising Sun on Abbey Lane.

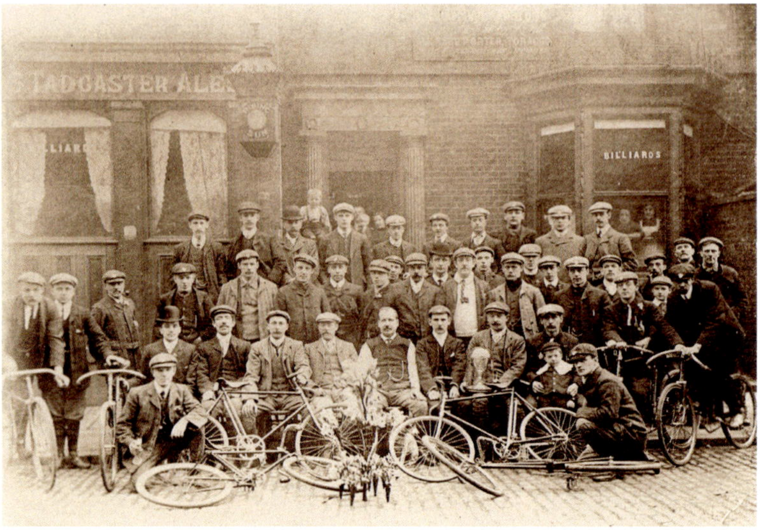

The cycling club outside the Rising Sun on Abbey Lane in the early 1900s.

Another significant event in the pub's history was when, on 4 July 1993, the pub's manager was attacked by two thugs armed with revolvers. Landlord Margaret Haywood and three staff members behind the bar were overpowered and tied up with a washing line. Publican John Haywood was in his office when the men broke in, squirted him in the eyes with lemon juice and struck him on the head with a gun. The thieves escaped with several thousand pounds in cash from the day's takings – a celebration of the USA's Independence Day.

The pub today is thoroughly modernised, though it still hints at ancient origins. It is a rather upmarket drinking and eating establishment.

The Hammer & Pincers, Ringinglow Road, Bents Green

The lovely old pub is situated on what was the western boundary of Sheffield and on the route of the major turnpike road out of the eighteenth-century town. Until the 1700s, lying to the west would have been the unenclosed expanses of heathy common land. By the 1800s the parliamentary enclosures took the common from the commoner and pushed the moorlands up the hill. A blacksmith located here would no doubt pick up good passing trade from travellers and travelling tradesmen. These were potentially thirsty customers so, in the early 1800s, the local blacksmith at this site in Bents Green introduced a taproom to his forge. The present pub is a descendent of that enterprising blacksmith, with the name the Hammer & Pincers reflecting its smithy origins. The complex of cottages here was, in the seventeenth century, home and workplace to the Osborne family with the main building used as a blacksmith's forge. It was part of this building that in the 1820s became a pub and the old forge gradually fell into disrepair. The modern pub serves good food and excellent beers. It describes itself as an historic stone-built pub, nestled between the edge of the Peak and the city – one of the most recognisable in Sheffield.

Close by at Thrift Cottage, is one of the oldest living things in the whole of Sheffield and the surrounding areas – an ancient yew of indeterminate age. Sadly scorched by a

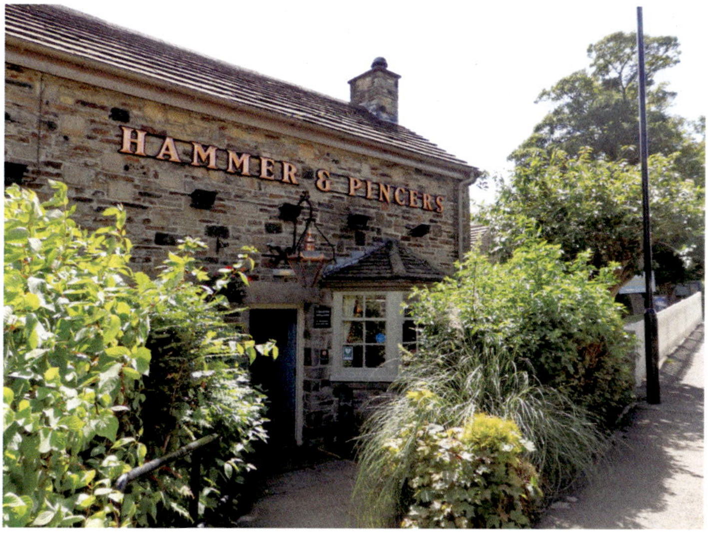

Hammer & Pincers inn sign.

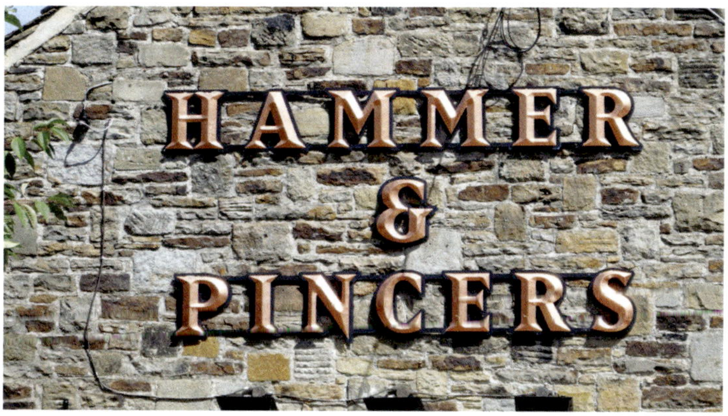

Metal Hammer & Pincers letters on the side of the building.

fire some decades ago, the ancient tree now protected by a Tree Preservation Order still clings on and was perhaps located on a formerly significant ancient boundary in the countryside.

The Banner Cross, Ecclesall Road

The Banner Cross Hotel is a good Sheffield locals' pub, one of the few left with a traditional taproom, attracting mainly a regulars' crowd along with a number of students and real ale drinkers. The Banner is a traditional pub with three rooms and a large beer garden to the rear. The lovely wood-panelled lounge is the quietest of the three rooms with the jukebox turned down low and is the main room used at lunchtimes for dining. The Taproom is the main bar area for sport with two plasma screens, one of which shows sports in 3D. Upstairs there is a pool room with a pool table and another two big screens. The jukebox in this room is louder and there is a separate bar (used for big nights) so that a pint is never far away! The Banner Cross public house was named

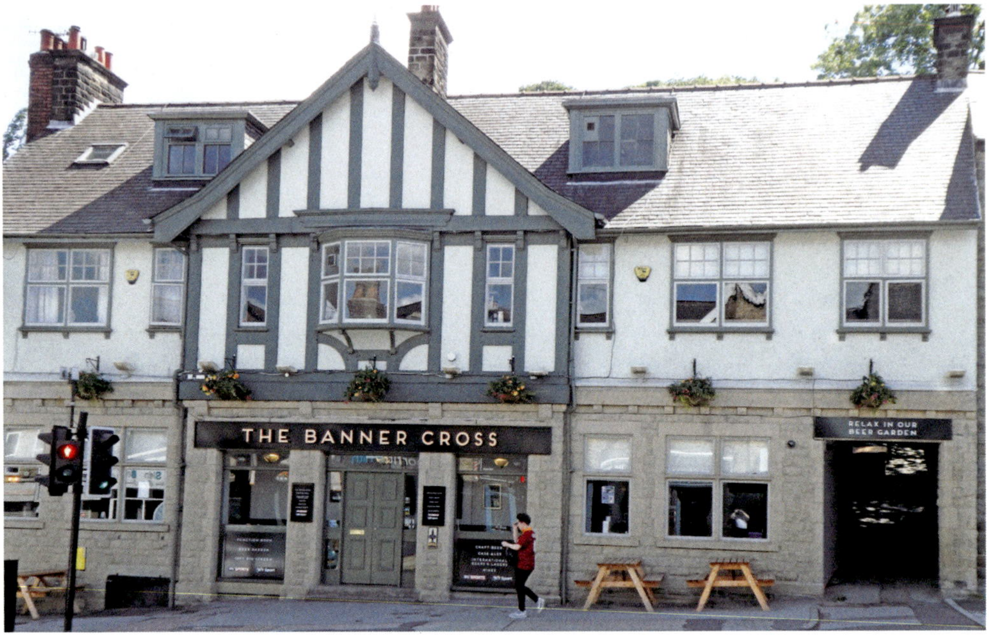

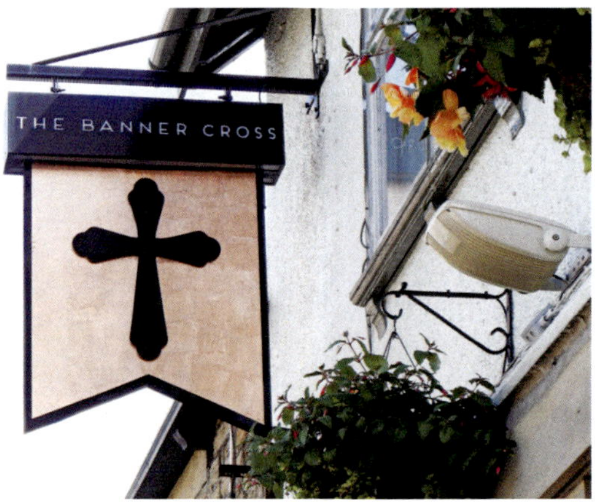

Above: The Banner Cross.

Left: The Banner Cross inn sign.

after a cross that was situated in the area some hundreds of years ago. There is only one other pub in England (in Torquay) called The Banner Cross.

A good few rogues will have frequented this hostelry over the years, but none more dastardly than one in the late nineteenth century. Located on one of the main routes from Sheffield centre to the west, this old Sheffield pub has connections to the story of the area's most notorious villain – cat burglar and murderer Charlie Peace. This was a man who was a burglar, bigamist, fence (stolen goods dealer), an adulterer, and because of his eye for the ladies, eventually a murderer. (His womanising is perplexing as he was a singular unattractive individual!) He lived two separate lives, one in Sheffield and the other in London. He further complicated things by forming a relationship with a Mrs Dyson who lived close to his house in Darnall. However, when Mr Dyson suspected something was amiss he moved his family to a house at the side of The Banner Cross public house. According to Ron Clayton, it was at Banner Cross that Charlie Peace fixed on his future mistress, Mrs Katherine Dyson. Mrs Dyson was described as an attractive woman, 'buxom and blooming' with dark hair and about twenty-five years of age.' From the first 'brief encounter', a series of events unfurled that led to the fatal shooting of the lady's long-suffering spouse, the six-foot five-inch Arthur. This occurred just below The Banner Cross Hotel although the site was redeveloped quite recently. The unfortunate cuckold, Mr Dyson, arrived home finding Charlie and Mrs Dyson in a compromising situation. In the resulting affray, Dyson chased Peace out of the house and continued his pursuit into the passage that runs at alongside The Banner Cross Hotel. Halting the pursuit, Peace turned on Dyson with a revolver in hand and shot. The betrayed husband, Dyson, fell to the ground, mortally wounded.

Peace made his final will dated 7 February 1879 while at Armley Gaol in Leeds. He left his possessions to 'my dear wife Hannah Peace now residing with my son-in-law William Bolsover, of Hazel Road, Darnall.' Just before his execution for this murder, Peace admitted to another killing prior to the death of Mr Dyson, that of a police officer in Manchester, PC Nicholas Cock. A double murderer, he was also the most famous cat burglar in Victorian England. It took the jury just twelve minutes to convict Peace of the murder in Sheffield of Arthur Dyson at Banner Cross in 1876 and he was hanged on Shrove Tuesday, 25 February 1879.

Today, with a wide clientele ranging from eighteen years to eighty, The Banner has a warm trouble-free atmosphere. The popularity for sport doesn't change this, with football matches being extremely well attended. Whether you like a pint with friends, a bite to eat or a venue for sport, The Banner Cross has it all.

The Greystones, Greystones Road

The Greystones describes itself as the flagship pub for the Bakewell-based Thornbridge Brewery, a welcoming, traditional community pub where people of all ages can enjoy a great range of drinks in comfortable surroundings. Perched near the top of Greystones Road, this pub was built as the Highcliffe in 1939. Since that time it has had more than a few famous characters through its doors. Joe and Fred Davis, both world champions at snooker and billiards, used to practice at the Highcliffe. Today there are cask ales from Thornbridge's award-winning craft ales and beers on tap, together with lagers and a wide range of bottled beers. In its former incarnation as the Highcliffe, this large estate pub, situated halfway up a very steep hill, was a well-known venue for music from the 1960s and 1970s onwards. At that time the Highcliffe Folk and Blues Club hosted musicians such as Billy Connolly, Mike Harding, Barbara Dickson, Ralph McTell, John Martyn, Duane Eddy, John Otway, Joe Brown, and Al Stewart. The regular MC was local star and BBC Radio Sheffield presenter, Tony Capstick. With one of the authors, members of local bands such as Heaven 17 and the Human League frequented the old Highcliffe as under-age drinkers in the 1970s. This was before heading down the hill to 'Shades' discotheque. The new owners, Thornbridge Brewery, have put the venue back on the map, turning it into an excellent place for food and drink and a venue for music and events too.

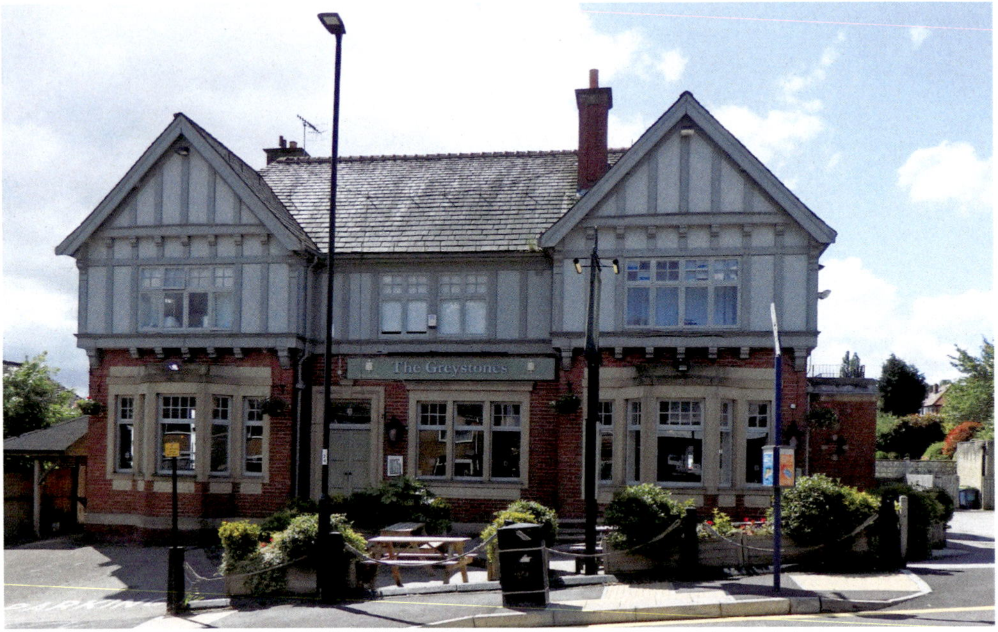

Above: The Greystones on Greystones Road.

Below: The Backroom music venue within the Greystones public house.

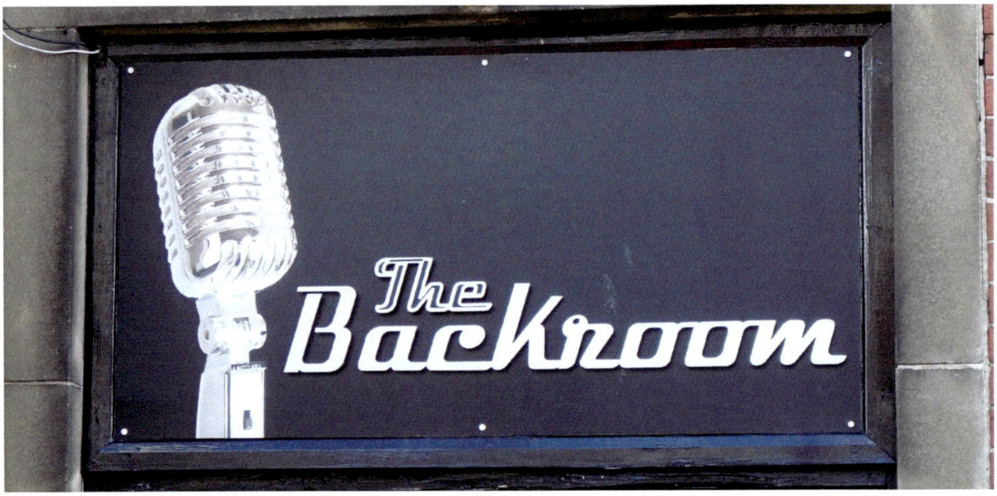

The Greystones public house is now an icon for the local music industry, with bands or groups, duos and solo artists performing many nights every week. Indeed the Greystones is now probably the top venue in Sheffield for music at the more affordable level. These gigs are performed in The Backroom – a great venue for professional entertainers with plenty of space for seating and dancing. The performers gracing The Backroom, many in recent times, range from the local groups such as The Everly

Pregnant Brothers through to the likes of Hawley & Simpson, the Wilko Johnson Band and many more.

The Greystones is a welcoming, traditional community pub where people of all ages can enjoy a great range of drinks in comfortable surroundings. Cask ales from Thornbridge's award-winning range are on tap, alongside quality lagers and an extensive variety of bottled beers specially selected by our brewers.

The Stags Head Inn, Psalter Lane

This rather distinctive old pub replaced an earlier and reputedly decrepit beerhouse from the late 1600s. Owned by Revd Alexander MacKenzie, he had the old establishment demolished and new premises built, opening in 1805. The location was a good one for customers being situated on the historic Psalter Lane, a salt route from the west into Sheffield centre, and by this time, the turnpike road. The MacKenzie

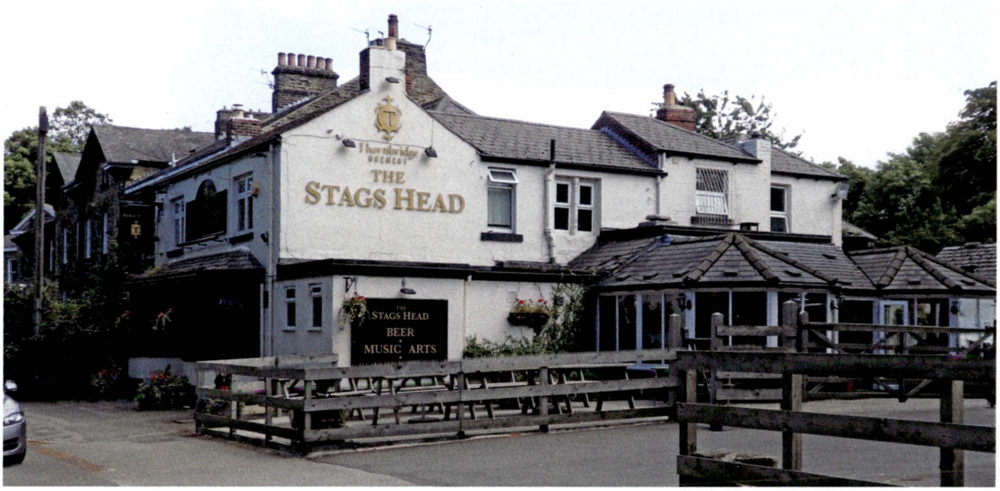

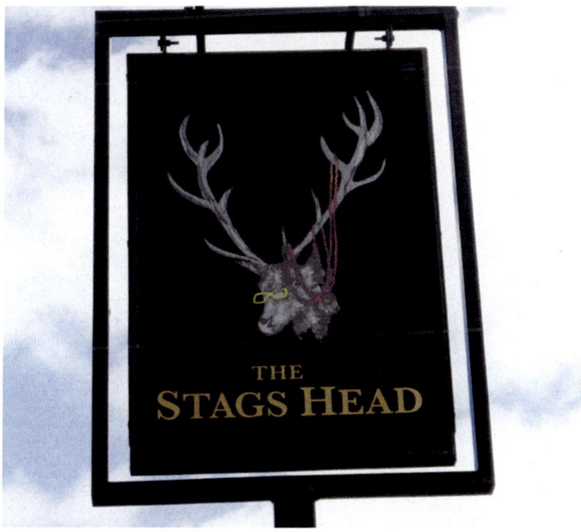

Above: The Stags Head, Psalter Lane.

Right: The Stags Head pub – a more comical sign.

family crest boasted a stag, hence the name of the new pub. The present-day Stag inn was constructed at the rear of the original site when the 1800s building was itself demolished. Close by, at No. 189 Cemetery Road by the grand Victorian General Cemetery, there was a 'MacKenzie Tavern', perhaps on the site of the first building. The pub is now an outlet for the Thornbridge Brewery called The Stags Head and offers good food and drink.

The Pointing Dog Clubhouse, Ecclesall Road

Better known to many older folk as the 'Polish Club', this has long been a venue for meetings, activities and general socialising. In recent years it has been refurbished and extended and has reinvented itself as a 'New York themed tavern' bar and restaurant and is now known as the Pointing Dog Clubhouse. It still has a function room and a stylish conservatory overlooking Ecclesall Road. It serves real ales and a range of beers but also now has an extensive range of cocktails as well as serving food.

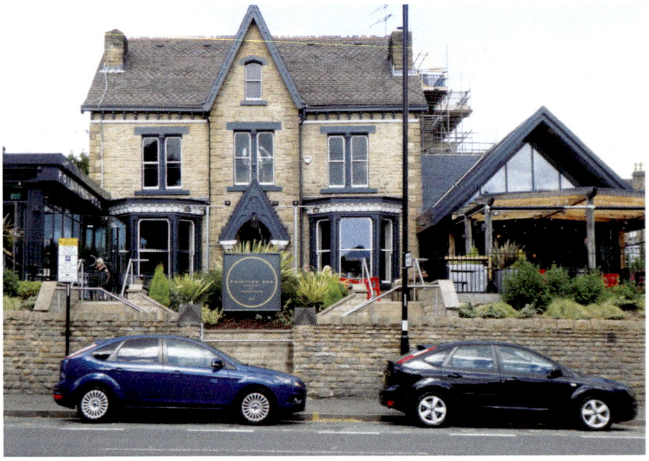

The Pointing Dog exterior.

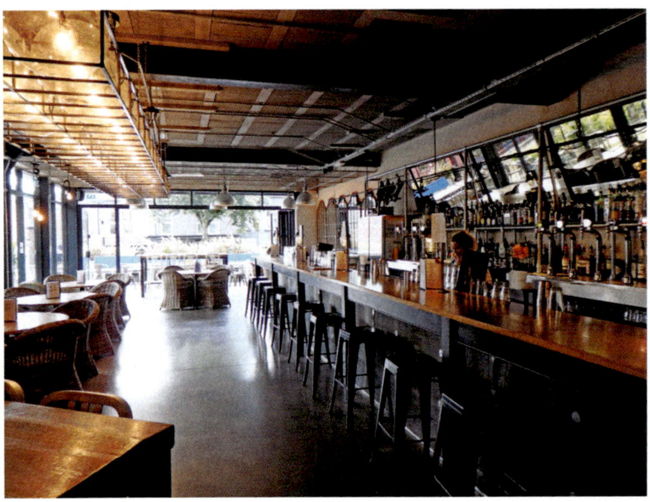

The Pointing Dog bar area.

This was originally the Polish Ex-Servicemen's Club. Its heyday was in the 1950s to the 1970s. It was set up after the Second World War, to become a focal point for members of the Polish community who settled in Sheffield rather than return to Poland after it fell under Soviet communist rule.

The Shiny Sheff, Crimicar Lane, Lodge Moor

This is a 1960s estate pub on the edge of Lodge Moor in western Sheffield, close to the Peak District National Park. The pub serves traditional food and good beers. The name has links to the three Royal Navy ships, destroyer class, which have been called HMS *Sheffield*. This name comes from the tradition of naming this class of ships after English cities and was chosen to honour the city as the home of high-quality stainless steel manufacturers. Hence the 'shiny' part of the pub name. The Shiny Sheff pub was built as part of the development of the area in the 1960s and 1970s, which is reflected in its design.

This is another of the pubs in this book with a unique name as it was specifically named after the third HMS *Sheffield*, a Type 42 guided missile destroyer, which was commissioned around 1970. There have been three Royal Navy warships named HMS *Sheffield* after the city and county borough of Sheffield, South Yorkshire:

1. HMS *Sheffield* (C24) (1936)
A Town-class light cruiser that saw service in the Second World War from the Arctic Circle and the Atlantic to the Mediterranean. She was one of the Royal Navy pursuit ships that tracked down the German battleship Bismarck. She was sold and scrapped in 1967.

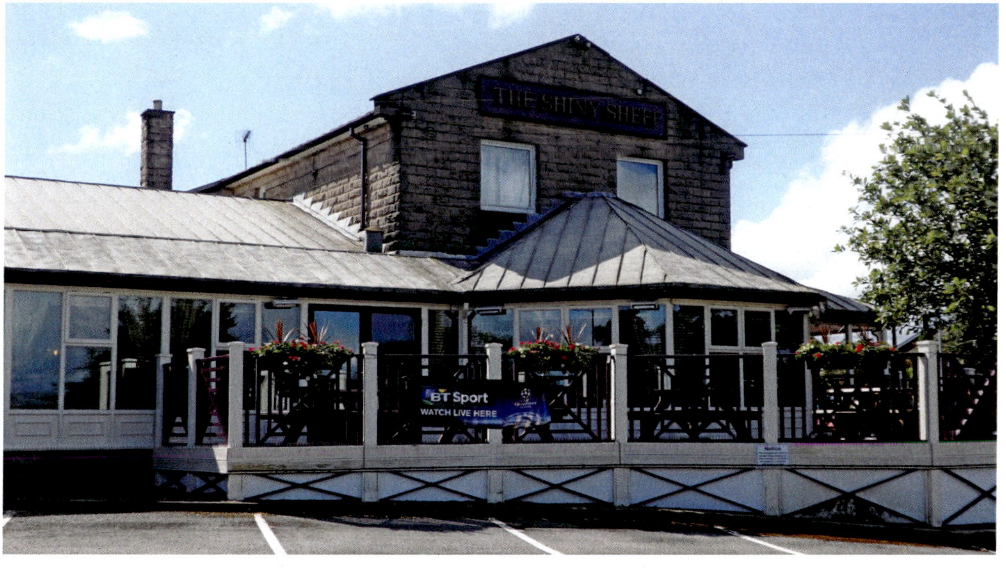

The Shiny Sheff named after HMS *Sheffield*. The ship included a great many stainless steel items, leading to the nickname 'Shiny Sheff'.

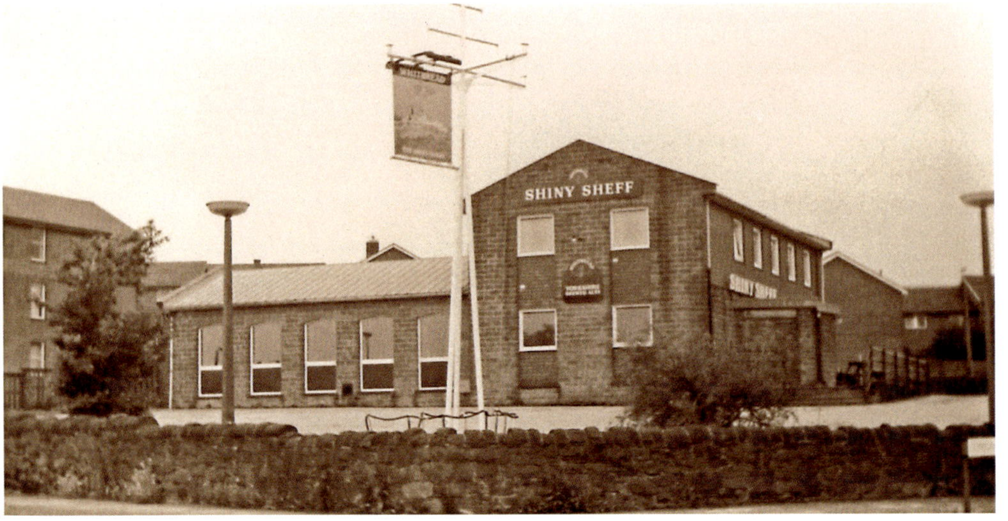

The Shiny Sheff in the 1980s.

2. HMS *Sheffield* (D80) (1971)
A Type 42 destroyer badly damaged by the Argentinian Air Forces on 4 May 1982 during the Falklands War. While being towed towards South Georgia Island, she sank in heavy seas.

3. HMS *Sheffield* (F96) (1986)
A Type 22 frigate sold to the Chilean Navy in 2003 and renamed *Almirante Williams*.

All three Royal Navy warships carried many fixtures and fittings manufactured in Sheffield itself. These included many stainless steel items leading to the nickname applied to them all, the 'Shiny Sheff'.

The second vessel became the most famous after being badly damaged in May 1982 after an Argentine air attack during the Falklands War, subsequently sinking. The name was allocated to a new ship in 1986, but since that was decommissioned and sold, the name has not been assigned to another vessel. Crew members from the ship and its replacements have visited the pub on an annual trip each year. The pub's decor includes pictures of the ships and other memorabilia. Its location also made it popular with people who visit the fringes of the National Park and the Lodge Moor and Wyming Brook areas for walks. The pub was recently closed for a period of refurbishment and revamped, with an opening in 2015 attended by local MP Nick Clegg.

The Fox House Inn, Hathersage Road, Longshaw

The Fox House Inn at Longshaw is a country pub in the heart of the Peak District National Park. It is described as oozing rural charm and rustic character, with picturesque surroundings providing the perfect backdrop for savouring the hearty, seasonal pub-food on the menu, carefully nurtured cask ales and fine wines gracing

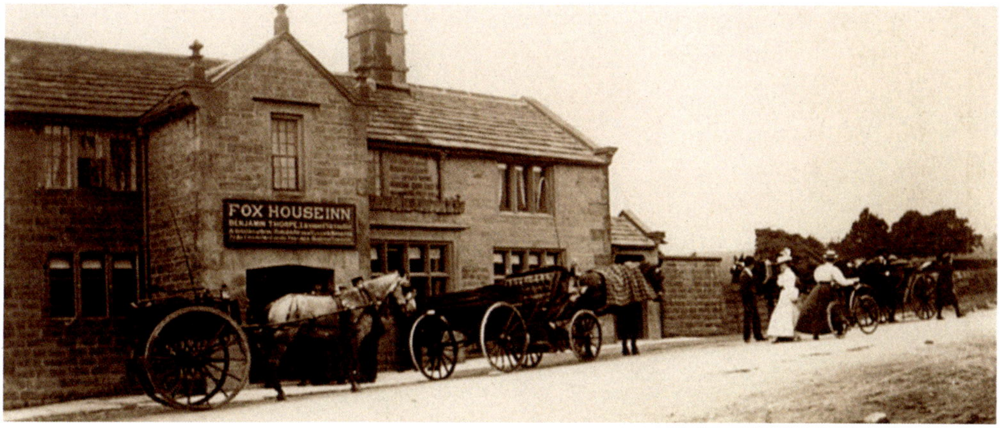

Above: The Fox House Inn, Sheffield, early 1900s.

Below: The Fox House sign.

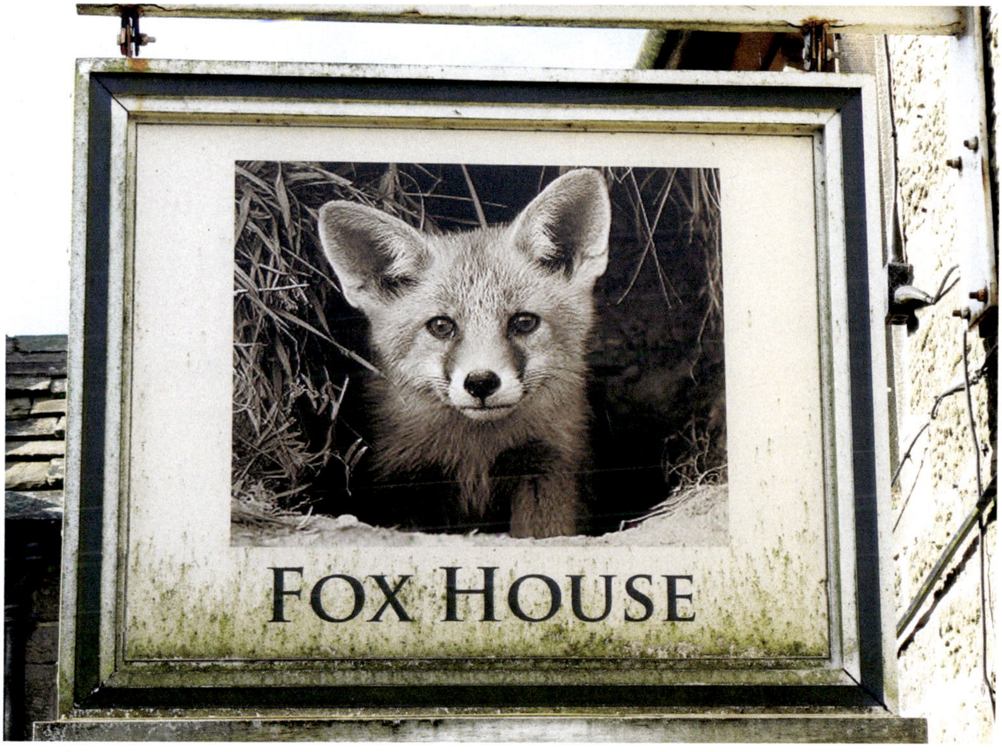

the bar. In recent decades the place has diversified and boasts ten good rooms for accommodation of tourists and for business meetings. The pub was originally part of the Longshaw Estate, formerly owned by the Dukes of Rutland (now the National Trust). The large bottom room was known as 'The Duke's Room' because the eighteenth-century Duke of Rutland sometimes slept there.

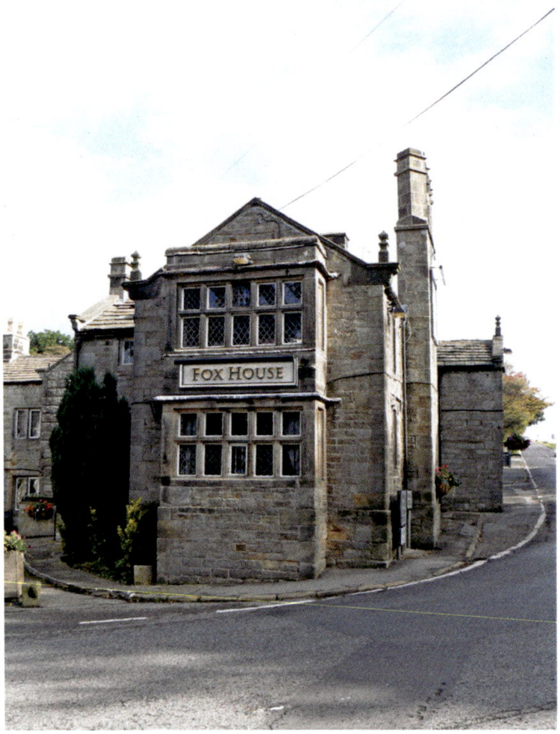

The Fox House inn.

While most people assume the pub is named after the fox, that is not the case. This eighteenth-century coaching inn was named after Mr Fox of Callow Farm in Highlow, who may have been an early landlord. Highlow in Derbyshire was described in the 1800s as 'a lordship in the parish of Hope and Bakewell union, 4 miles south-east from Hope and 3 miles south-west from Hathersage. Highlow Hall formerly belonged to the Eyre family. The acreage is 421; rateable value £326; the population in 1881 was forty-four'. The land in Highlow was mostly owned by the Chatsworth Estate – the Devonshire family and not the Rutlands as at Longshaw. The building at Fox House dates back to 1773, but was extended by the Duke of Rutland, as the landlord in the 1840s. Lying close to the summit of long hauls up either Hathersage Road from Sheffield, the turnpike road to Buxton, and Sheffield Road out of Hathersage, the inn was a favourite resting place for livestock drivers and the passengers of stagecoaches.

Bulmer's *History and Directory of Derbyshire from 1895* notes that 'Longshaw, near the Yorkshire border, is a shooting box of the Earl of Rutland, and near here, on the Sheffield road, is Fox House Inn, a noted hostelry still, and even more famous in the old coaching days'. Furthermore, the views close by were remarkable, 'The surrounding scenery is extremely beautiful with one view, called The Surprise, surpassed by few in the county.'

By the early 1980s, the Fox House Inn would be packed with tourists and walkers, though the food was pretty basic with mostly burgers or pies and chips. Today's pub is part of the Vintage Inns chain and has a broad and tempting menu to suit.

Chapter Five

From Crookes and the Rivelin Valley Across Northern Sheffield

The Ball Inn, Crookes

This is a large, early twentieth century drinking place in an area that has grown as a residential suburb over the last two centuries. It is on the site of the building of a much earlier licensed premises. The Ball Inn is now a flame grill and craft ale pub with fourteen different cask ales and traditional food. The venue also hosts events and special feature evenings such as music. In the 1940s, the local butcher apparently sold horsemeat (which was still quite common at the time) and the local shop or perhaps a temperance bar near to The Ball Inn sold Vimto and Sarsparilla. Close by was a tram stop and a cobblers. This area, once famous for its heather moorland (Crookesmoor), became a heavily populated part of Sheffield during the late 1800s and early 1900s. The nearby open space, called the Bolehills, was a medieval site for lead smelting and it is likely that soils across the whole area still have some level of lead contamination.

The Ball Inn opened in the early 1800s in a building that previously was a farm with a beerhouse attached to it. The 1856 Directory of Sheffield notes Joseph Skelton as a licenced victualler of The Ball Inn and George Skelton of the same address, as a 'Cowkeeper'. This is hardly surprising since these hostelries were often family enterprises and included a number of different businesses. Additionally this was still a time when, with an expanding local community, there was a need for dairy farms or at least milk cows almost as far as the town centre. Immediately prior to this period Crookes was still a largely rural, farming village. As the urban area spread and travellers were heading west out of Sheffield, there would also be a need for hospitality and for stabling for horses. Although in the early 1800s The Ball landlords were the Skeltons, it was previously John Johnson, who was notable for boarding apprentices

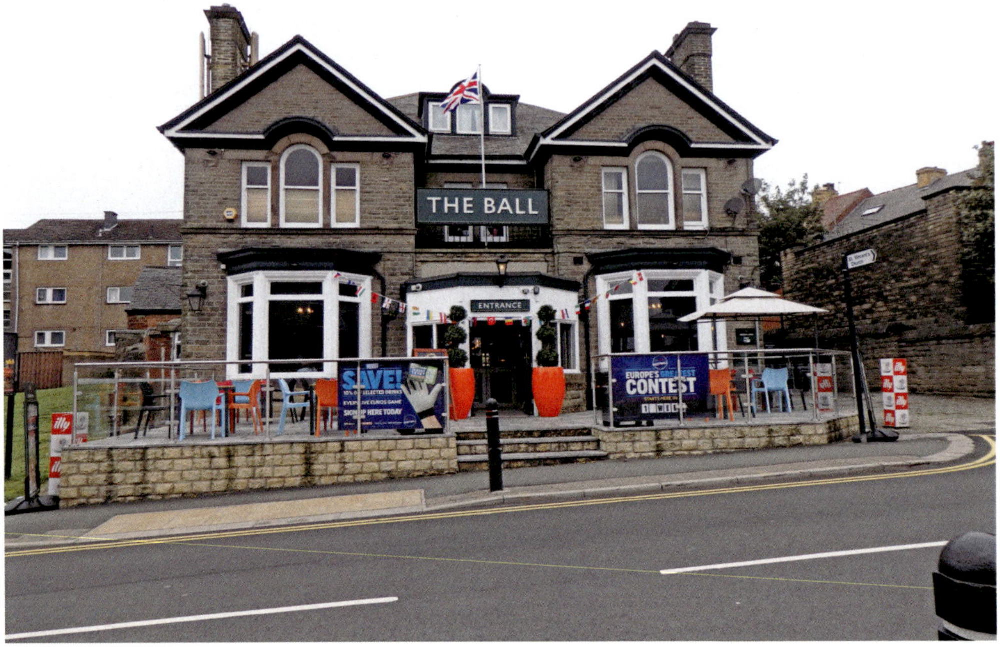

Above: The Ball Inn, Crookes.

Below: The nine-seater settee – ideal for large parties.

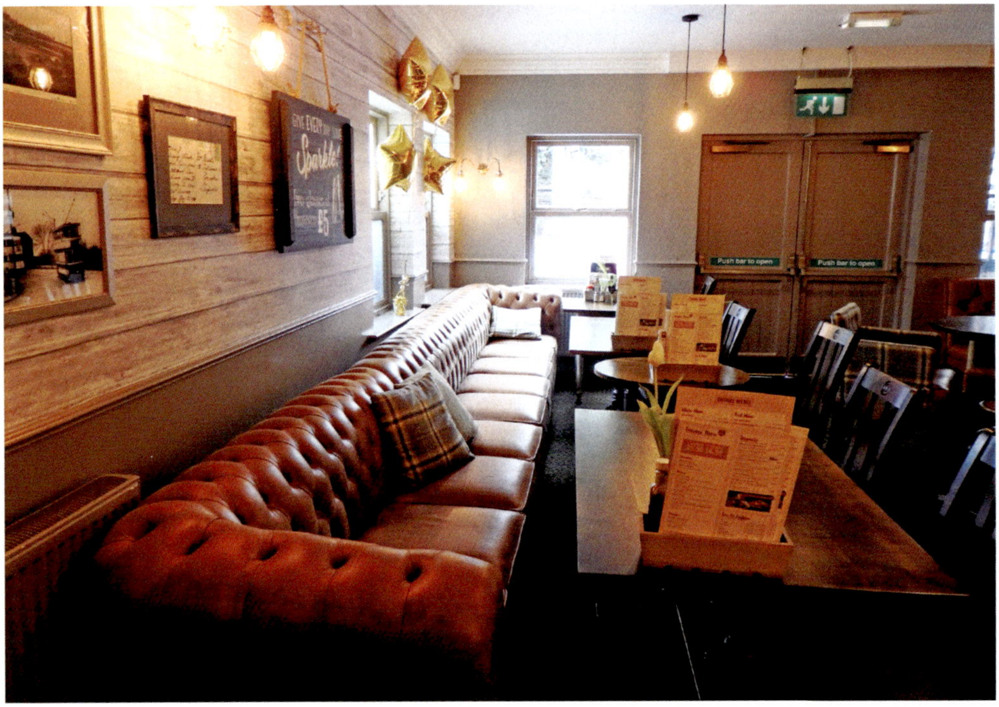

and feeding them on poor porridge. The result was that they rebelled and threw their wooden spoons and bowls into the fire. Apparently the food subsequently improved! It seems that the earlier buildings were demolished in the late 1800s or early 1900s, and the modern pub replaced those.

We believe this is one of the most frequented public houses in Sheffield. The place is always very busy, whether visiting at dinnertime, evening or even early mornings. Joanne, the manager of this large pub, keeps wonderful, newly refurbished premises that can cater for hundreds of drinkers and still has plenty of room for customers to sit and eat a nice meal in peace. However, when there is a football match being shown on the large television screens of the local team, Sheffield Wednesday, it may be best to order your meals early. It can become a little, shall we say, lively. Nevertheless, other than the three or four times per season that the Owls appear on Sky TV, The Ball Inn is a nice, open plan, large restaurant pub that will make sure you enjoy your visit.

It was extensively refurbished in the early part of 2016 and kitted out with new extra comfortable armchairs and large sofas, making The Ball Inn an ideal public house for large groups or family get-togethers. The seating in the dining area is well spaced out and we recommend you to try out the remarkable nine-seater settees; seek it out if you come to Sheffield.

The present-day Ball Inn was one of Sheffield's 'Bowling Green pubs' (it has its own bowling green). The locals would play between 12 noon until 2 p.m. closing time. They began again at 7 p.m. until darkness fell on summer evenings. This may be where the name for the pub has come from, with the sign of the bowling ball indicating its sporting connection. However, another possible derivation for 'Ball' especially Blue Ball in the local area, was the suet pudding made from local bilberries. The pudding, which was round in shape, turned bluish after cooking. Some local pubs put these delicacies on their menus and the pub name reflected this. Bilberries were once common on local moorland.

The Cobden View, Cobden View Road, Crookes

The name of the public house comes from Richard Cobden (1804–65), a Corn Law reformer. He was an English textile manufacturer, an alderman of the newly formed Manchester Corporation, and a radical and liberal statesman associated with two major free trade campaigns, the Anti-Corn-Law League and the Cobden-Chevalier Treaty. In 1838, Cobden and Quaker radical John Bright founded the Anti-Corn-Law League, aimed at abolishing the unpopular Corn Laws, which protected landowners' interests by levying taxes on imported wheat, therefore raising the price of bread. In this context from 1841, as a Member of Parliament for Stockport, he fought against opposition from the Peel ministry, and abolition was eventually achieved in 1846.

Situated on Cobden View Road, the public house is well over 100 years old, which can probably be surmised from the period stone frontage. The Cobden is a real community pub that has events most nights including barbecues, weekly acoustic nights and various quizzes. The 'Cobby' is a very traditional old-style pub with a warm and friendly atmosphere situated in the heart of Crookes. The building is a cosy, unassuming stone-built Victorian building of considerable charm. This is a very welcoming pub and

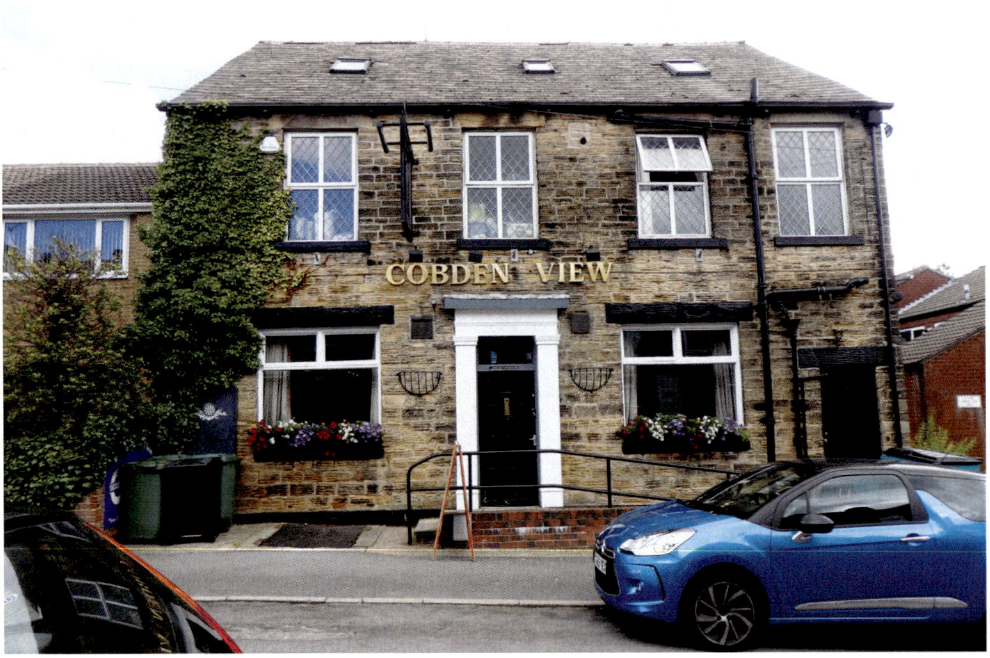

Above: Cobden View, sited on Cobden View Road.

Below: The bar in the pool room.

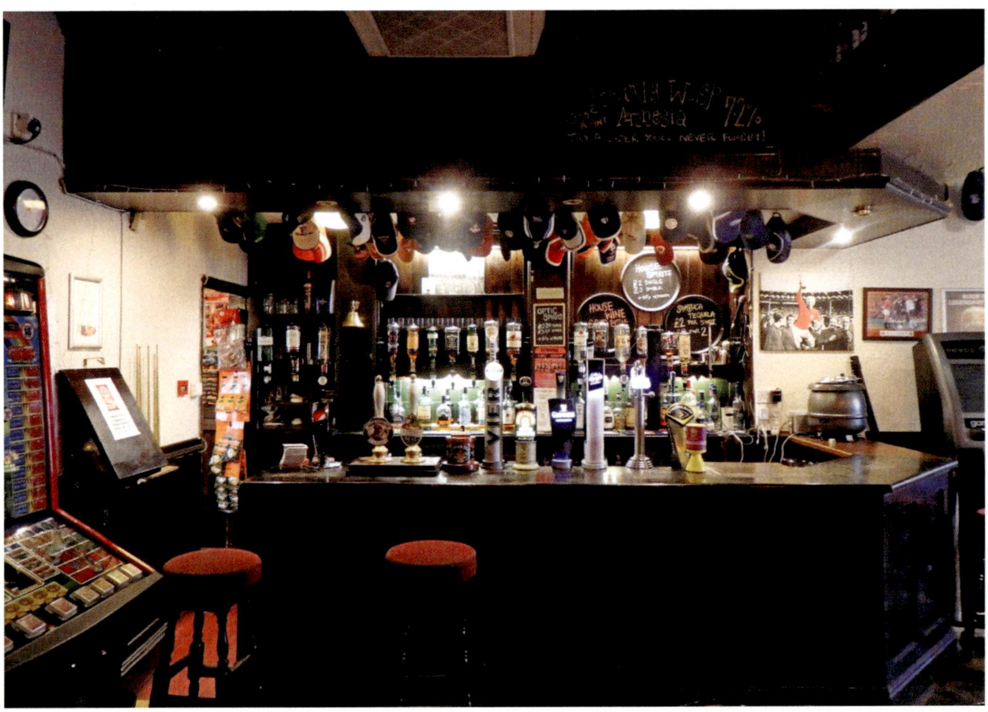

customers are a mix of students, professionals, sports teams and people of all ages. The Cobden prides itself on what it claims is the best pool table in Crookes, kept so with regular care and maintenance. They host regular pool competitions and knockouts. It is also the home of the Sheffield University Bankers Hockey Club.

The Cobden is a safe, family-friendly community pub that offers great beers (including a CAMRA special), lagers and ciders as well as a range of events and activities to suit families and students alike. With full Sky, Sky Sports and ESPN included, there is also always plenty of sport on offer.

The Rivelin, Tofts Lane, Stannington

The Rivelin is a lovely, cosy, countryside public house set on Tofts Lane, a high point in the lower Rivelin Valley. This is a solid-looking, stone-built Victorian building that originated at the time of the industrial Rivelin Valley with its water-powered mills and works. In July 2010, this historic but unassuming little pub was bought by a local neighbour and subsequently refurbished and reopened. The pub now serves food and drinks, including the local Bradfield Brewery beers. Furthermore, the renovation has been done very tastefully to keep the feeling of history. The pub is now convenient for the Rivelin Valley Trail and other local walks – as long as you don't mind a fairly steep hike from the valley bottom to the south-facing hillside on which The Rivelin is perched.

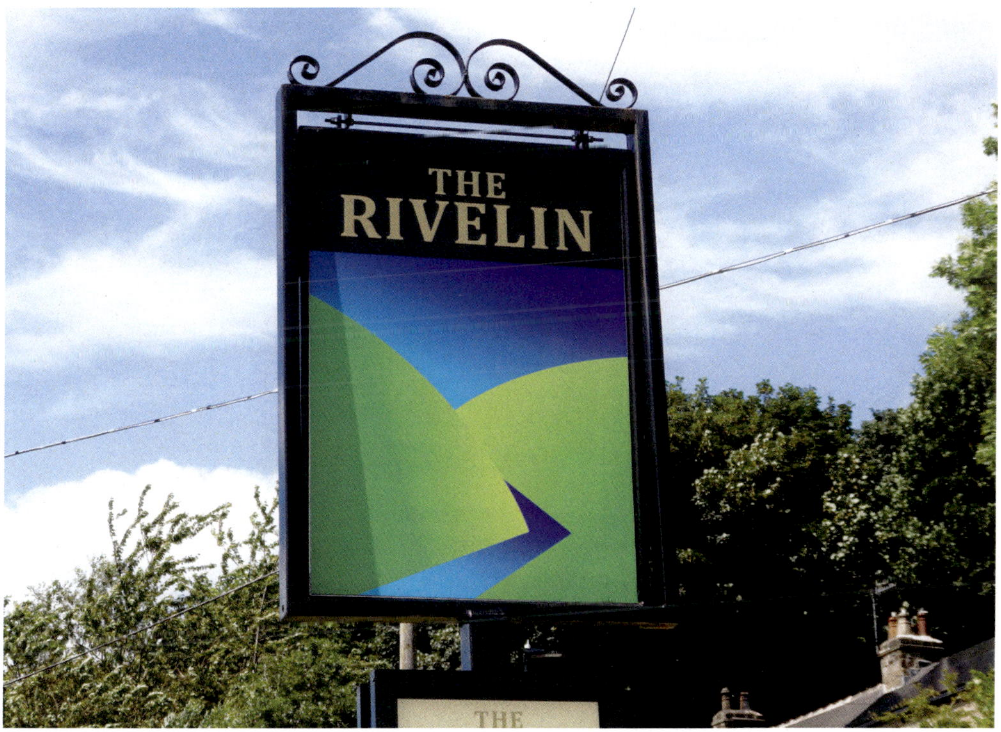

The Rivelin public house sign.

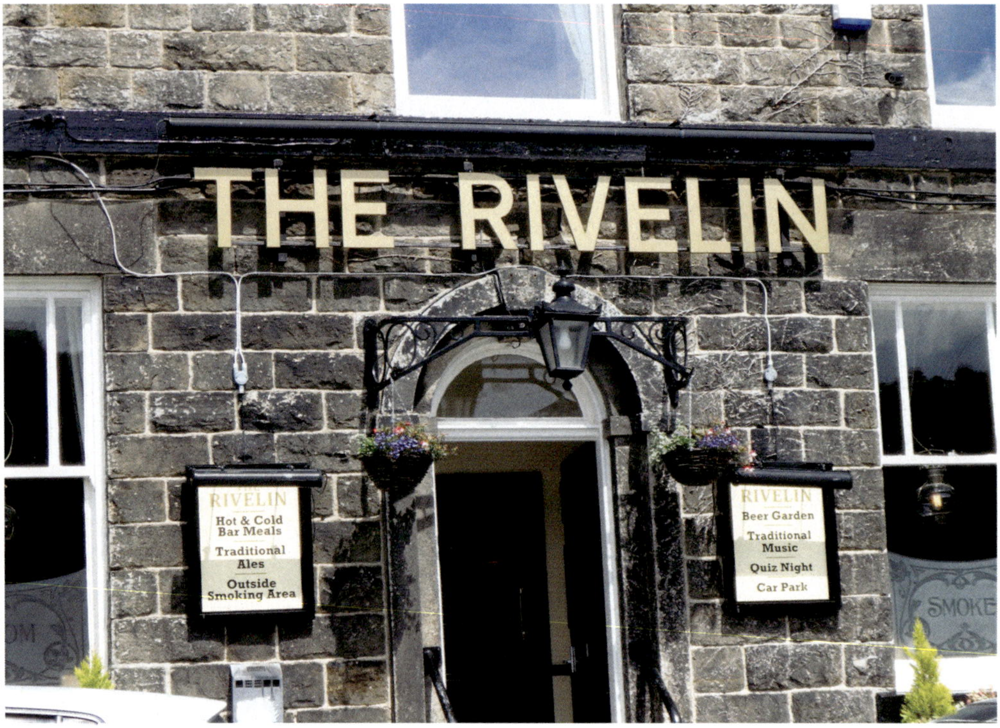

The Rivelin hotel sign over the front door.

The gritstone building was constructed in 1850 as a mill cottage and was converted into a public house a few years later. It has a stunning view over the Rivelin Valley and is just a short, steep walk from Stannington Village. On that walk you will pass the Man's Head Rock that overlooks the pub. Years ago the lounge was nicknamed 'The Surgery'. It apparently got its name when the regulars used to meet and discuss their ailments over a pint. That seems a really good way to treat your health problems ... having a pint. It may not cure you but you might forget you are ill!

The Rivelin is not one of the new-fangled 'gastro pubs' but the sort of place that existed before chain pubs became ubiquitous. Yes, this pub has had some money spent on it to give it a modern look, but the building proudly retains its history. The home-cooked pub grub is not only excellent but great value with generous portions and prompt and friendly service.

The Closed Shop, Commonside, Walkley

This is a great little pub once part of the Donald Gilmour and Co. holdings, with a long-standing tradition of being cosy, busy, and welcoming. However, in June 1963, the atmosphere was rather less welcoming when, after the transfer of the licence from the landlord Mr Colin Fletcher to a Mr Philip Mulvaney, the premises were unexpectedly closed and not reopened. When barman Harold Bunting turned up for work he found the place closed and deserted. The landlord's wife and two daughters had left a

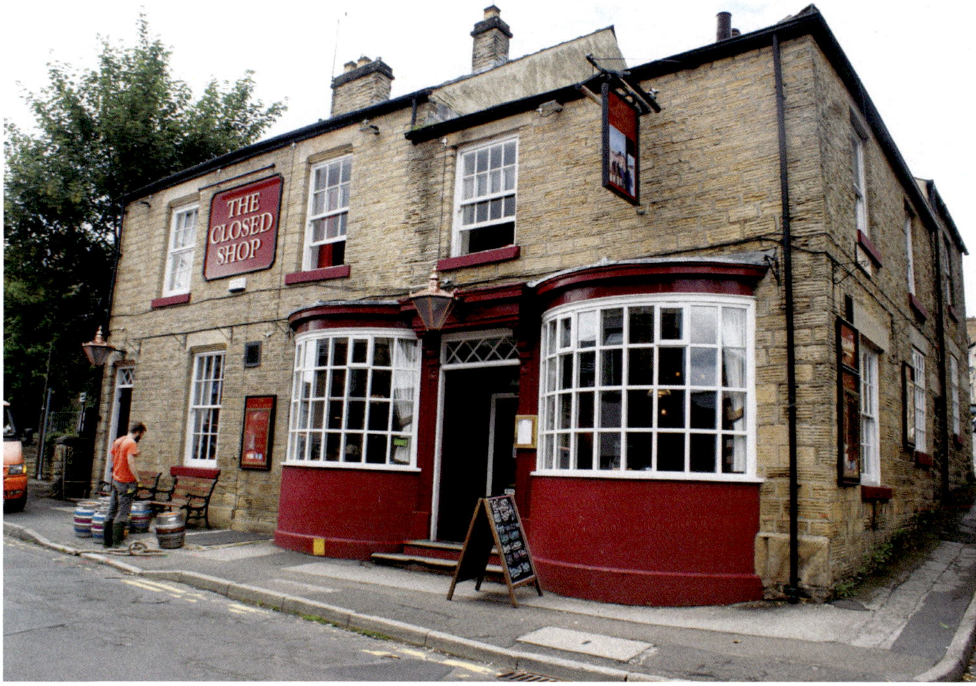

Above: The Closed Shop taking a beer delivery.

Below: The Closed Shop pub sign.

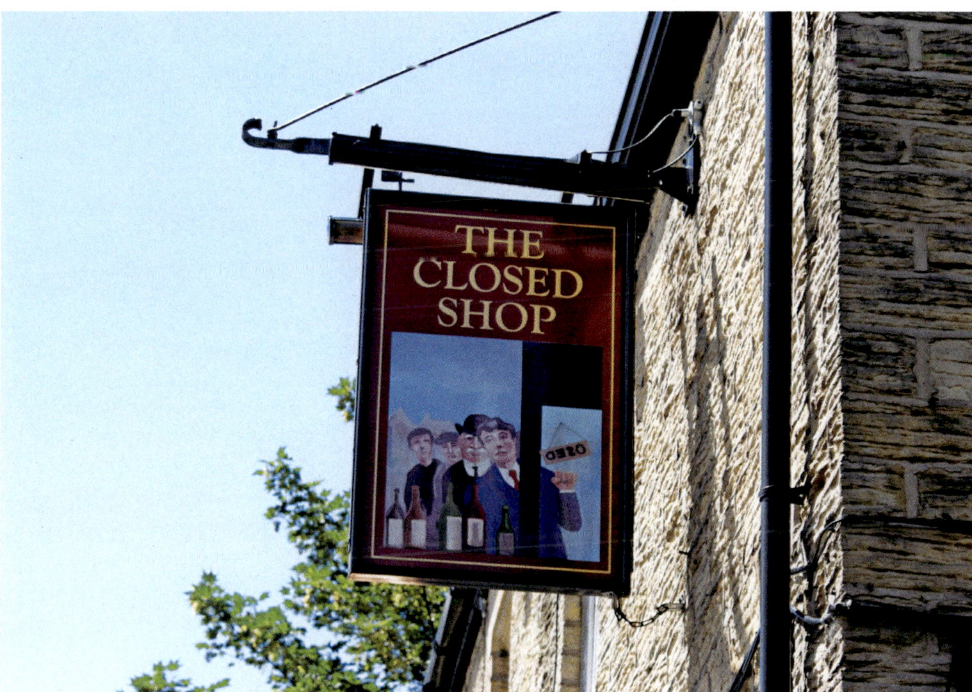

fortnight before and now both he and his personal effects had also gone. No reason or explanation was offered, but when *The Star* newspaper interviewed Mr Fletcher at a hotel in Castleton, he stated that he had finished with the licencing trade and wanted a fresh start. The pub survived the upset and with landlords such as Harry and Lee Watson in the 1990s, remains today a favourite hostelry for locals and students alike.

The Hallamshire House, Commonside, Walkley

This welcoming, traditional community pub, at the time of going to press, is managed by Becky and Tom Ashfield. All their staff offer excellent customer service and product knowledge. Cask ales from Thornbridge's award-winning range are on tap, alongside quality lagers and an extensive variety of bottled beers specially selected by their brewers. The pub offers regular quiz nights and a programme of live music, as well as the only full-size snooker room and table in Sheffield.

A couple of reviewers on Facebook sum up The Hallamshire perfectly: 'Always a good atmosphere. Decent prices, good booze and friendly staff. Live music nights are fun. Beer garden is a good, large covered area outside. Definitely recommend.'

'I used to spend a fair amount of time in here when Les May was the landlord. Really like the new look though as the new owners have preserved the real pub atmosphere whilst introducing a fresh classy decor.'

The Hallamshire House was originally a coaching house in the nineteenth century and stood facing the old manor Spring Farm, which was bordered by the farm workers' tied cottages although there is not much in evidence today that this was once a very open area of rich farmland.

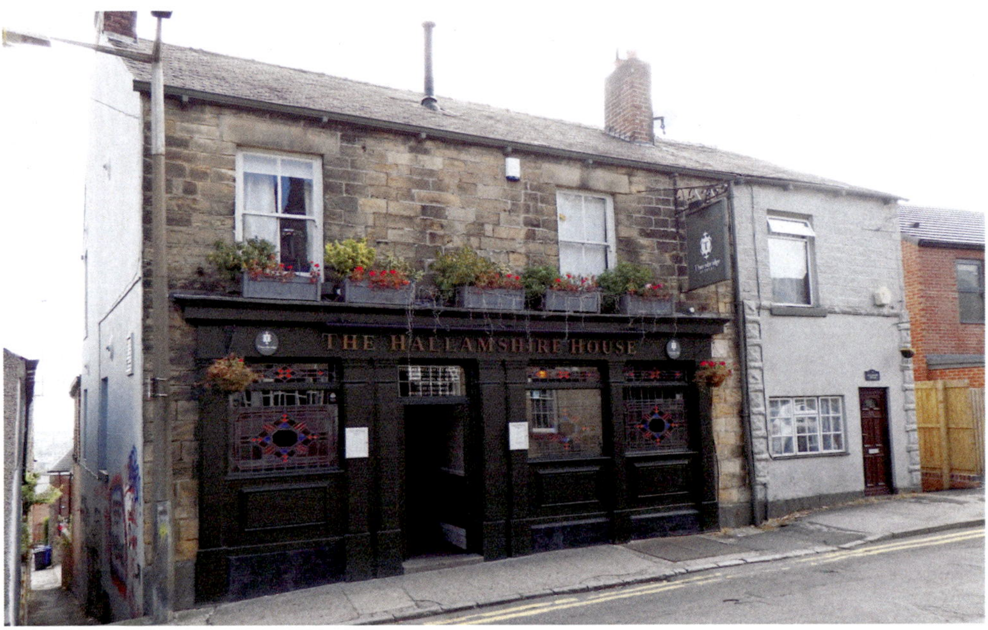

The Hallamshire House, Commonside.

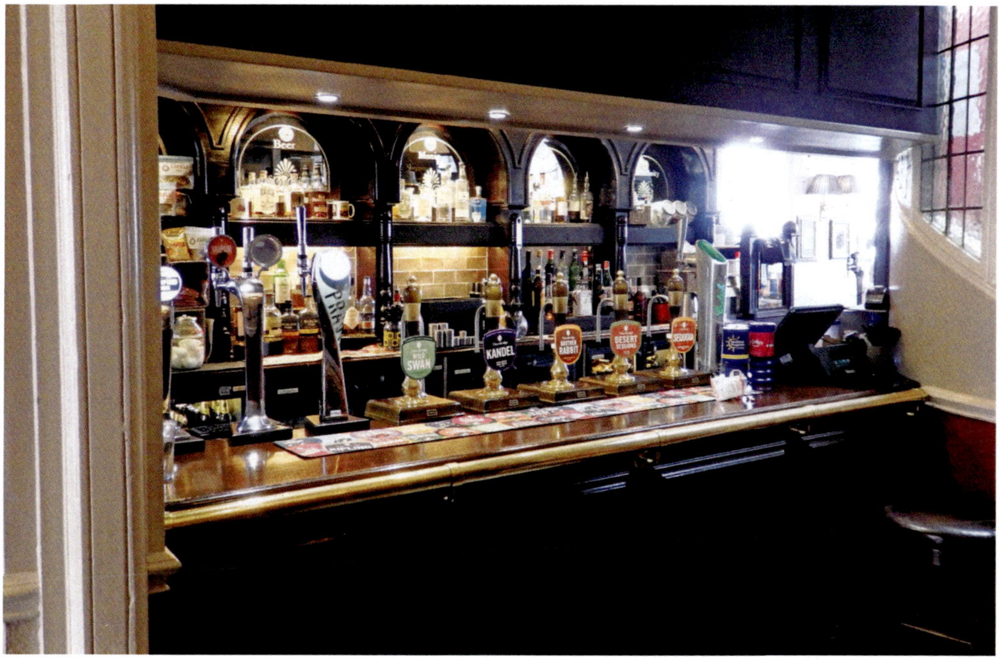

The Hallamshire House bar.

The Rawson Spring, Langsett Road, Hillsborough

Situated close to the banks of the River Loxley, this former swimming pool is now a Wetherspoon's pub so you can expect decent food and beer at very competitive prices. It is an interesting use for the one-time Hillsborough Baths and the nature of the historic building makes for a spacious 'open-plan' public house with a high ceiling but still a degree of interesting character, although few of the former features of the swimming pool are now in evidence. The outside facade still has the original name carved into it, although the pavement has been extended slightly to accommodate a Supertram stop.

The old Hillsborough and Walkley swimming baths was built in 1926 and was first turned into a public house in 1998; aptly named The Deep End. Around this time, every large building in Sheffield that came up for sale or was deemed surplus to requirement by Sheffield City Council (a bank for example) was being turned into a public house. The Deep End was one such project. The swimming pool area was converted into a seating area with tables and chairs, which were removed to create a dance area when the Deep End had gigs or other music events. The old, tiled changing cubicles were made into cosy little booths. However, times change and pubs lose their hold on the local clientele, and taste in the way the pubs are run also wane. This is what happened to The Deep End. Wetherspoon's, realising that The Deep End was one of the largest pubs in Sheffield, then stepped in. Wetherspoon's bought this almost-new pub and quickly set about gutting it. All the cubicles and tiling were removed. The large seating area that was supposed to hold over 500 customers was changed into a large open-plan

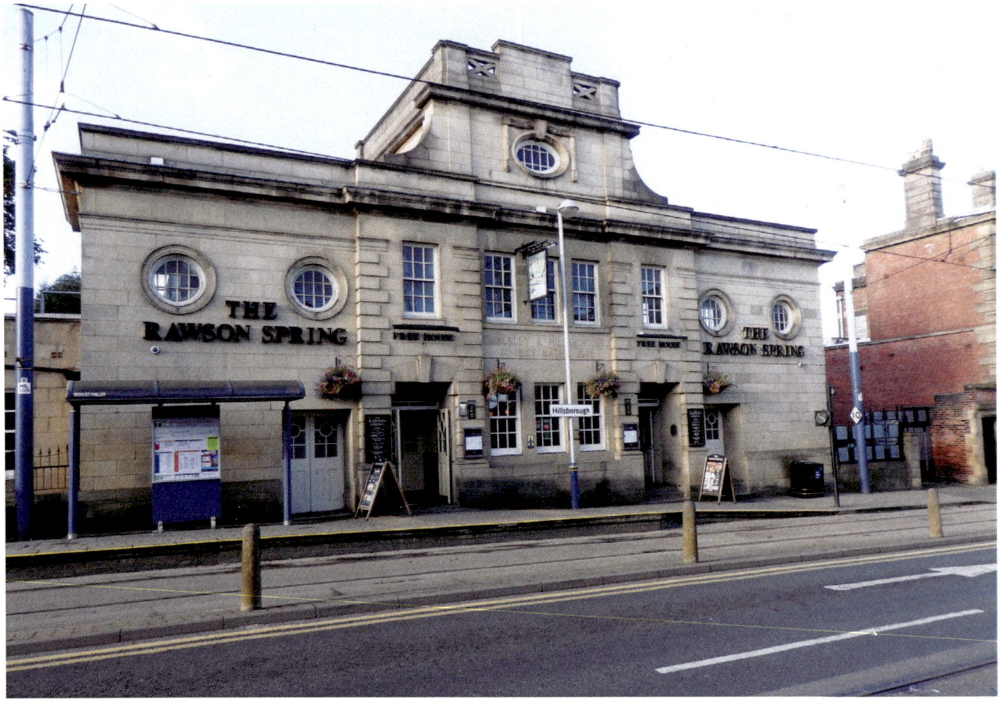

Above: The Rawson Spring at Hillsborough.

Below: The Rawson Spring interior.

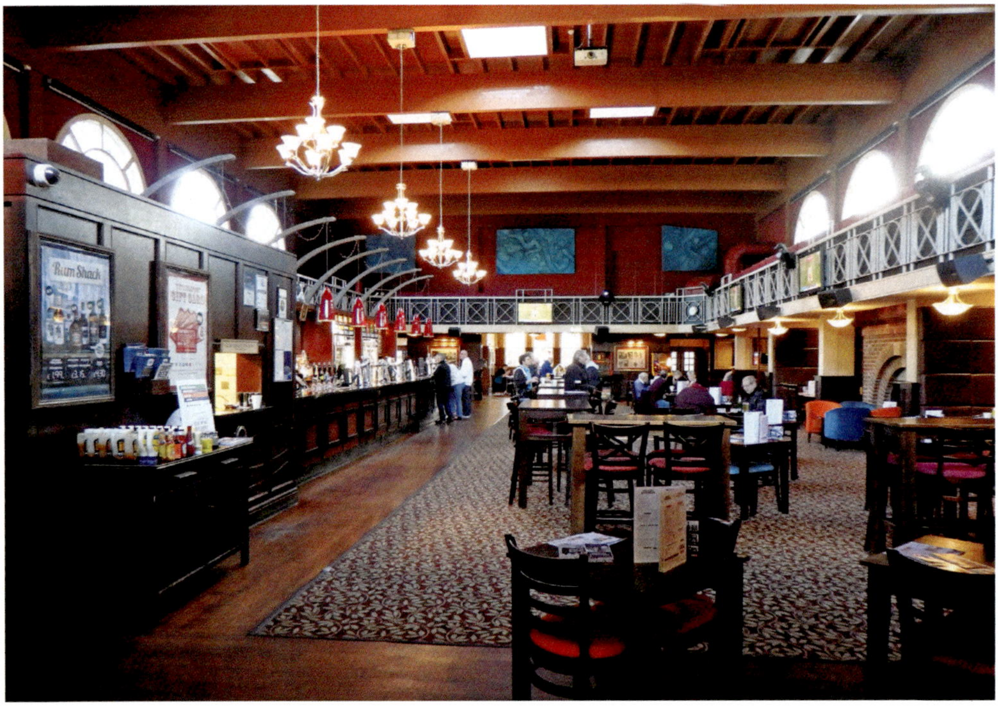

public house. It was renamed The Rawson Spring and like a phoenix from the ashes it has risen to become one of the busiest pubs in Sheffield. It is full to capacity every time Sheffield Wednesday play their home games at nearby Hillsborough football ground. It is almost as crowded on most Friday, Saturday and Sunday evenings. Throughout the warmer summer evening the excellent, large, beer garden at the rear can easily accommodate well over one hundred drinkers.

If you do visit, and we recommend it, try it on a 'non match day' at Hillsborough, unless of course you are an Owls fan.

The new name of the public house derives from an ancient woodland some distance away, on the hillside opposite at Parkwood Springs. Rawson Springs being a 'spring wood or coppice'. This is a type of woodland very common in the Sheffield area that formerly supplied charcoal and other products to support the local iron and steel industries. The Rawson family owned farms and tanneries in the Wadsley Bridge area for several hundred years up to the end of the nineteenth century. So the name of the pub commemorates not only an ancient industry but also a long-established family.

The Castle, Stone Moor Road, Bolsterstone

The Castle Inn was built in 1840 and is set within the richly historic parish of Bolsterstone, the name reputedly derived from two large boulders in the village. The area included an historic fortified medieval manor house and associated buildings, the ruins of which may be incorporated into the modern structures. Even then, the Yorkshire Pennine air had a reputation for good health as testified by a letter written by Gilbert, Earl of Shrewsbury, to his brother in law John Manners, dated 17 August 1587. This shows the earl obviously came to Bolsterstone for his health when he wrote 'I have come here to try if change of air will ease my gout'. The name of the inn clearly reflects this past heritage and the fortification. Furthermore, there seems to have been a hostelry here well before the present structure. For example, in 1627, Capt. Adam Eyre noted in his diary that he went to Bolsterstone to play 'bowles' but lost 7–6 on the game, spent *6d* on his dinner, and *4d* on ale. By 1907 Ann Bramall was the landlady, succeeding the previous landlord, her father-in-law Thomas Henry Bramall. The daughter of Joseph Grayson, a coal merchant and perhaps farmer residing at Leeke (or Leek) House on the Haywoods, Ann purchased the inn and '6 closes of land' for £4,750 in January 1907. In the 1960s the pub was still very traditional and busy with locals, especially at weekends. It was reputed that the barmaid at the time had well-muscled arms from having to hand-pull large numbers of pints. It didn't serve food at this time. The hostelry is now described as a large imposing open-plan pub with seating in the lounge around three separate serving areas and a games area. However, by the early 2000s the place had gone into a decline and despite a new landlord in 2007, the pub was not viable. Nevertheless, a change in management in 2013 has triggered a recovery under the ownership of Trust Inns. The home of the notable Bolsterstone Male Voice Choir is secure for now and the landlord, Les Kingstone, is working closely with the local community and others to rejuvenate activities in the village centred on The Castle Inn. There are plans for music festivals and other events to promote visitors to The area and vital customers to the pub, which now has a growing reputation for good beer and nice food.

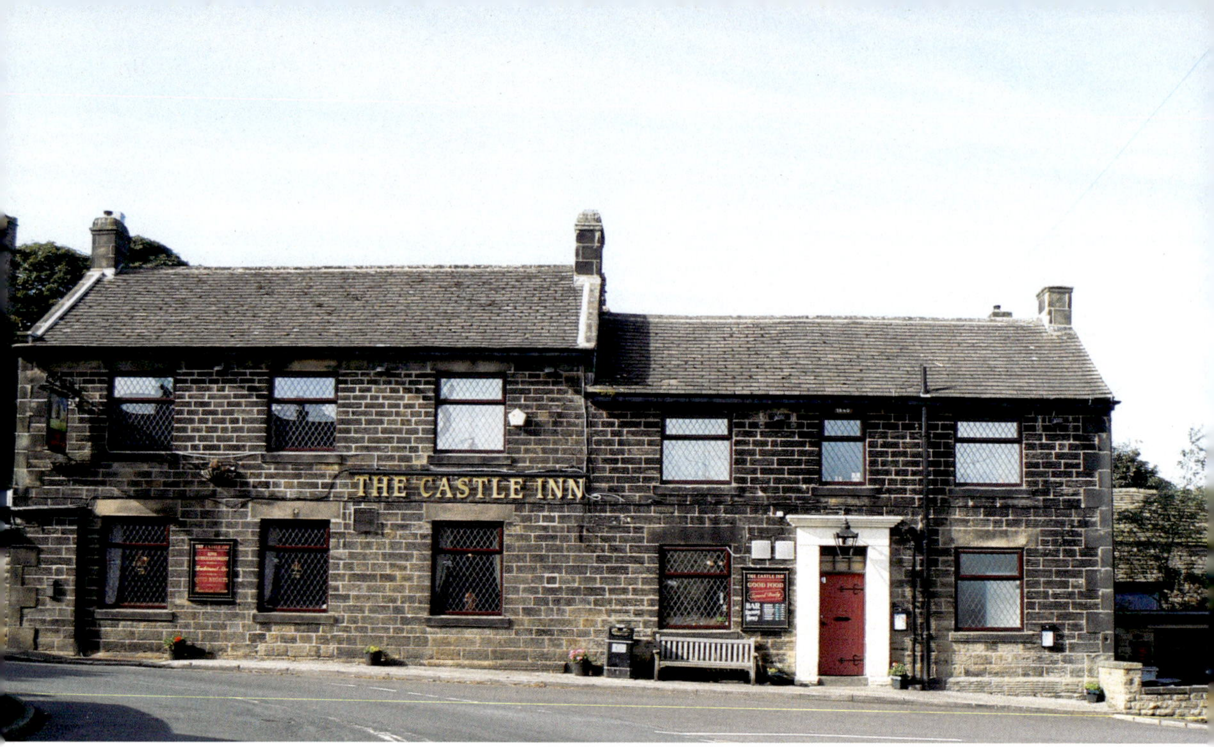

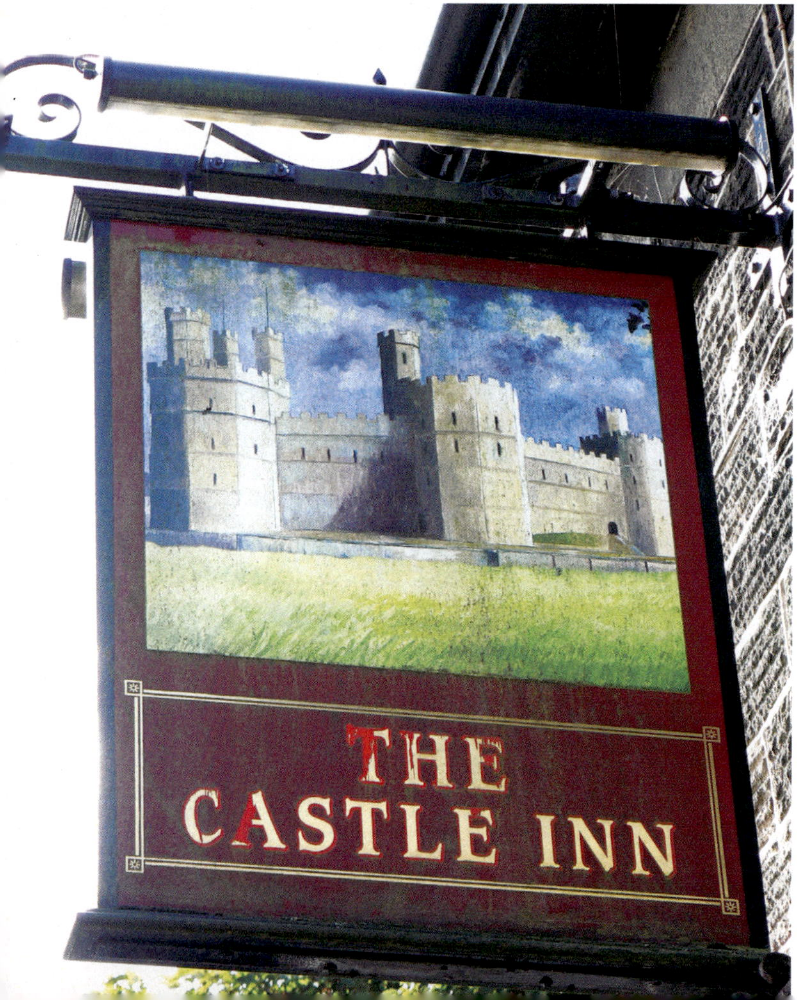

Above: The Castle Inn, Stone Moor Road, Bolsterstone.

Left: The Castle Inn, Bolsterstone, pub sign.

The Old Horns, High Bradfield

This wonderfully historic pub stands on Towngate, just opposite what was once (between 1759 and 1847) the Bradfield Parish Workhouse. The building is still there today, but its splendid features belie its historic use and the connections to the dire poverty of early industrialisation and the impacts of the 'parliamentary enclosures' on the landscape and community of this remote village. Outside the former workhouse, now private residences, is a file-maker's anvil or stithy. Boys in the workhouse were apprenticed to a trade and it is understood that the stithy was used in the workhouse. Bradfield Parish, meaning broad field or open countryside, is one of the largest such administrative districts in all England. It was once part of the even larger Ecclesfield Parish, which stretched from Rotherham to the Yorkshire/Derbyshire boundary. The view from the lounge and the car park must rate among the finest from any pub in the country with a panoramic view of the Loxley Valley and the scene of the terrible Great Sheffield Flood in 1864. The village boasts a Norman motte-and-bailey castle, Anglo-Saxon origins, and prehistoric features too. The church, which is mostly nineteenth century, includes much older buildings and the castellated building by the churchyard gates was a watch tower to guard against Victorian body snatchers.

The Old Horns has a direct connection to a particularly nasty incident in local history, the 'Kirkedge murder' in March 1782. Local man Francis Fearn used the pretext of

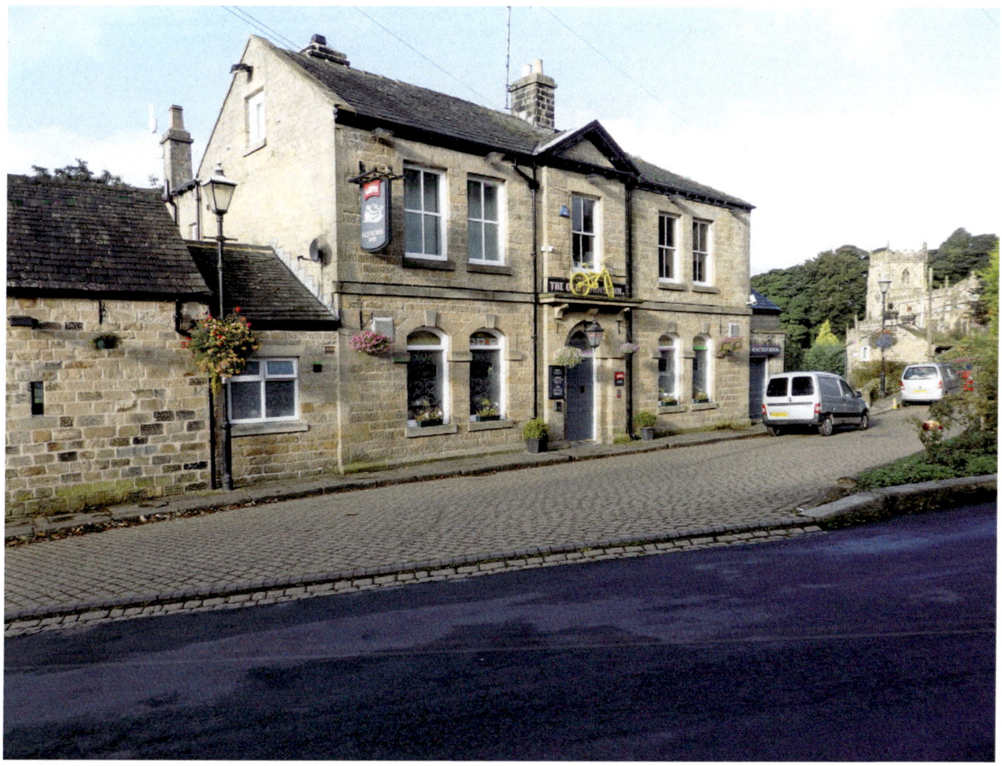

The Old Horns with Norman-era St Nicholas' Church.

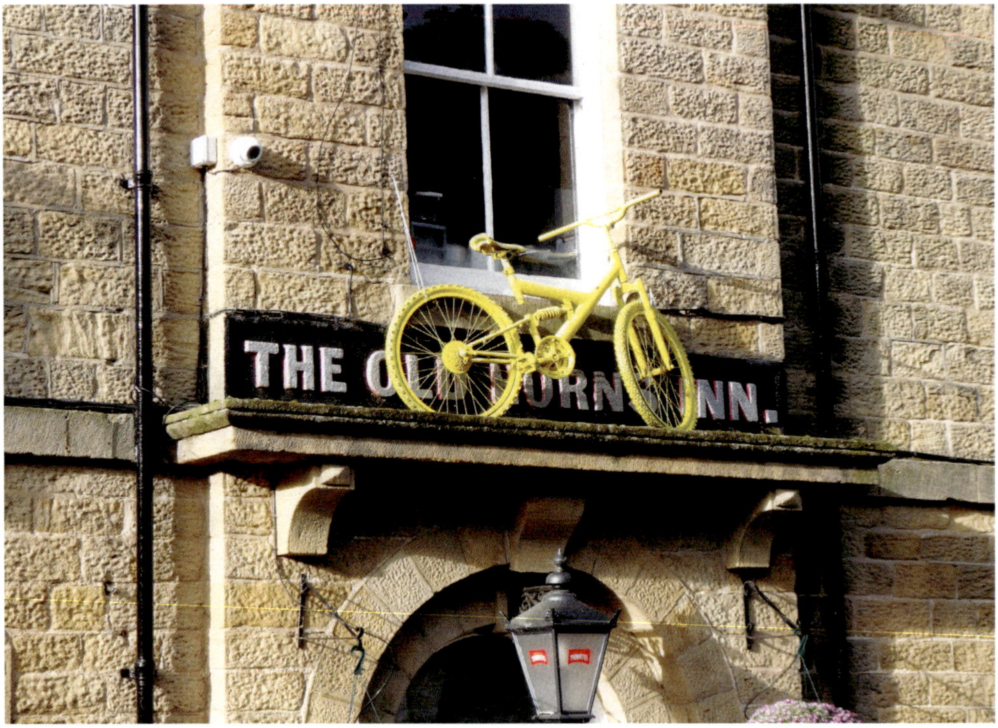

The Old Horns Tour de France route marker.

setting up a 'watch and clock club' at the Horns, something quite common at that time, where local people would contribute money each week until they accumulated enough to buy a timepiece. Fearn used this masquerade to entice Sheffield clockmaker Nathan Andrews to visit High Bradfield so the club might purchase clocks. However, the real motive was to attack and murder Andrews on the bleak and exposed Kirk Edge Road. The plan went wrong and after the body was discovered with its throat cut, Fearn was apprehended and confessed. After his trial and execution in York, his body was returned in chains and hung from a gibbet on Loxley Common. It is said that Fearn's last bones fell from the gibbet on Christmas day 1797.

The name The Old Horns or The Horns is quite common and often derived from Richard II's emblem of a White Hart. In the local context it may also refer to the hunting of deer on the nearby Loxley Chase.

Today, The Old Horns offers a spectacular location for good food and excellent beer. You can sit in the beer garden, take in the magnificent views and listen to the sound of the nearby church bells.

The Crown & Glove, Uppergate Road, Stannington

Perched at the top of the hill in Stannington on one of Sheffield's seven hills, it commands an excellent view of Sheffield and the Rivelin Valley. The Peak District can also be seen when looking west. Ex-landlord, Keith Ravenhall, once pointed out

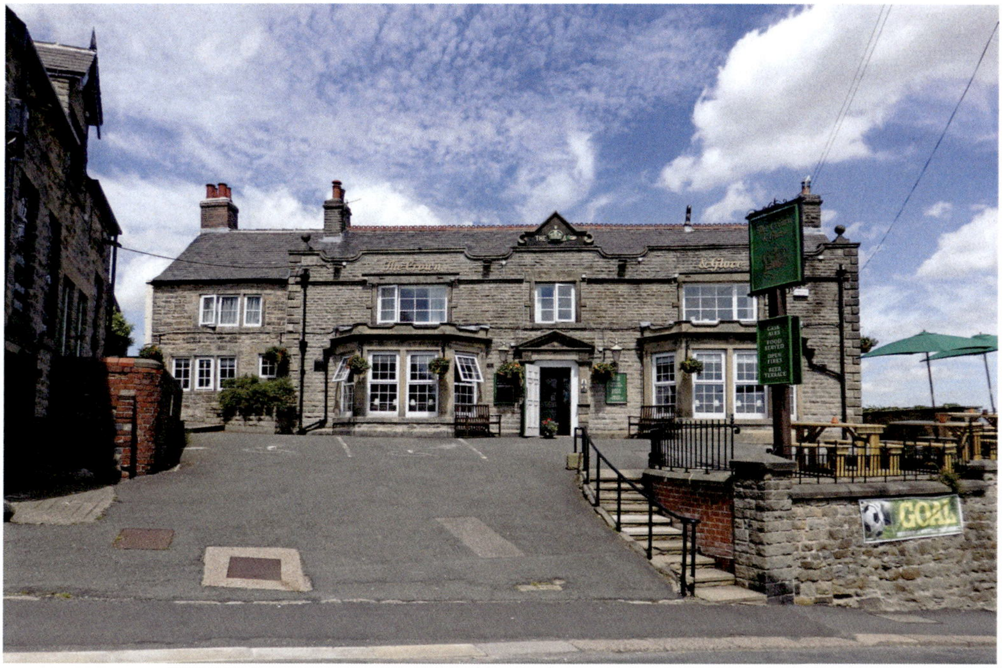

Above: The Crown & Glove.

Below: The Crown & Glove dining room bar.

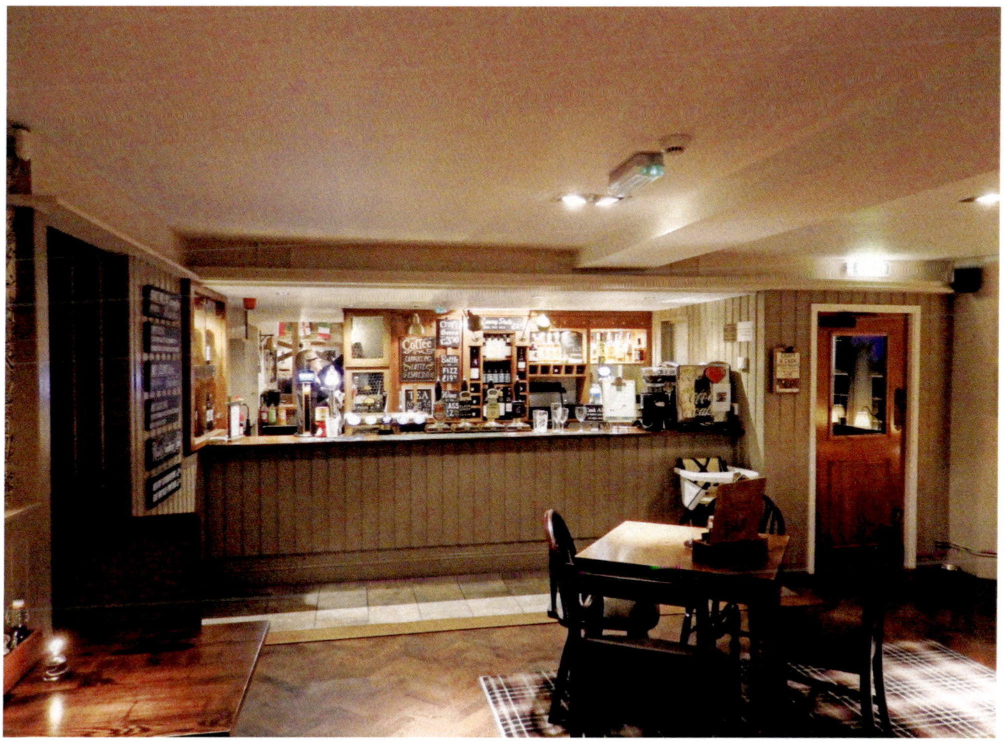

that the 'top house' is the highest point heading eastward until you reach the Urals 2,000 miles into Russia or whatever satellite they are in now.

'A particularly pleasant pub with a sense of well-being' is how it was described by the Royal Institute of Architects upon a visit while compiling a series of reports on public houses in the Sheffield area. Most of the regulars, there are a good few, would not argue with that statement describing this eighteenth-century coaching house. The pub was refurbished in July 2015 and now has all the facilities required to ensure you have a great experience when you are planning a night at the 'top house', as it is known locally. The suggestion is that The Crown & Glove was made into a public house by converting a number of cottages. It was then modernised in 1962, transforming it into a more comfortable pub and was used mainly by the local residents of Stannington Village.

Visitors are offered great locally sourced, freshly produced food, a great range of beers and wines and a warm welcome! Henry and Kitty are the incumbent landlords at the time of going to press. After its recent refurbishment it attracts diners and drinkers from far and wide who travel to enjoy the food, drink, and the excellent views that The Crown & Glove has to offer. The name 'Crown & Glove' is a reference to the gauntlet thrown down on Coronation Day daring anyone to dispute the right of succession.

The Peacock, Stannington Road, Stannington

The Peacock was first documented in 1828, the same year as Arthur Wellesley, the 8th Duke of Wellington, succeeded Lord Goderich as prime minister. Twenty-three years later, in 1851, George March – a blacksmith and farmer, was the licensee of The Peacock Inn. Then over the intervening 165 years it has served the small village

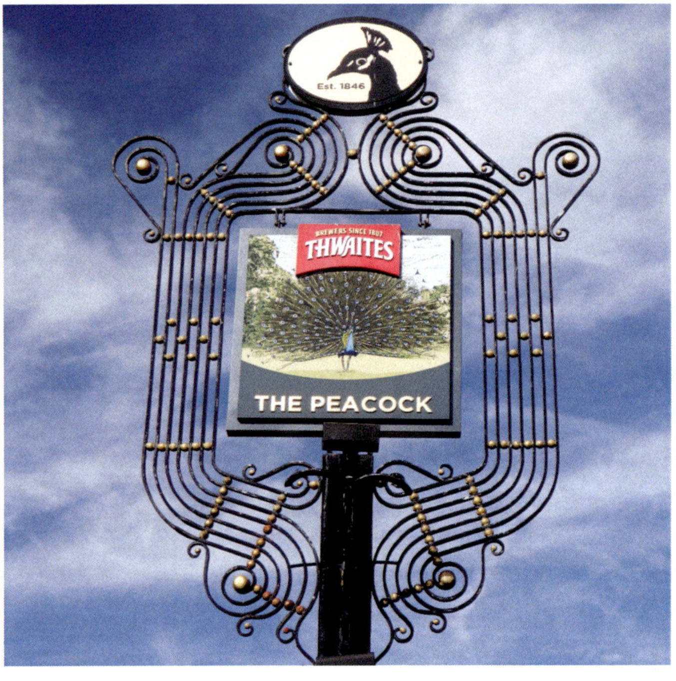

The Peacock sign.

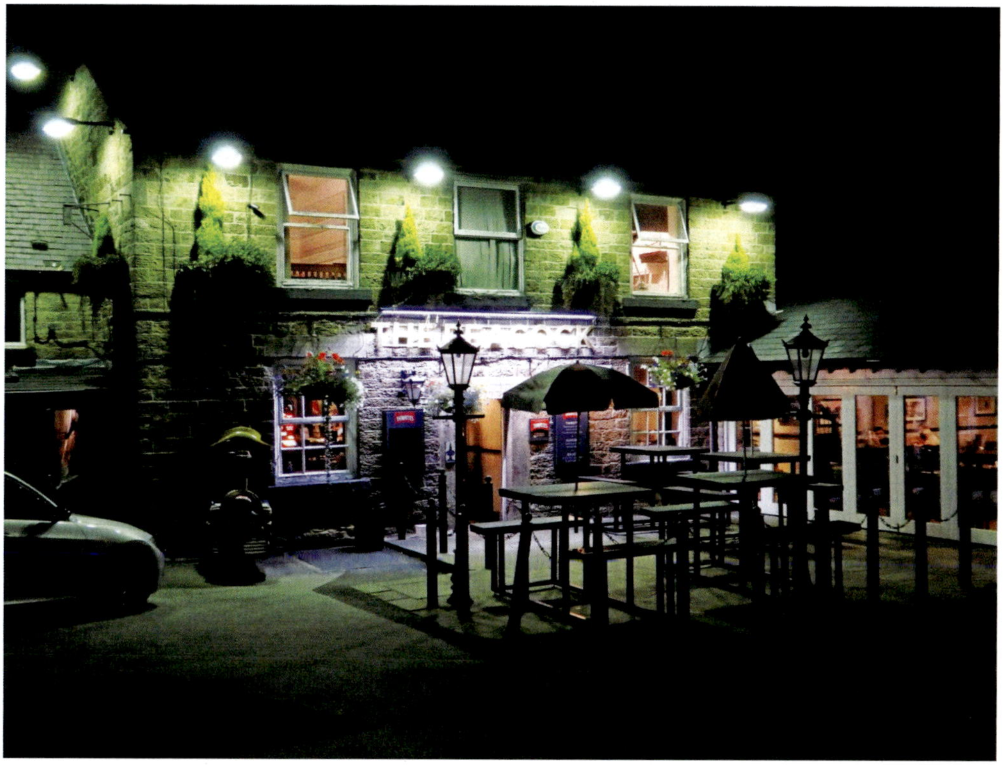

The Peacock illuminated at night.

of Stannington in the west of Sheffield very well. Located in the heart of the village, The Peacock inn offers what every traditional English pub should: a welcoming atmosphere, quality home-cooked food and a great range of ales. This public house is the perfect place to enjoy excellent food and drink with family and friends, whether you visit on their fun-filled quiz nights, a family meal or just to have a quiet pint – everyone is welcome.

The venue is a very popular food destination in the Sheffield area, thanks to simple, hearty, home-cooked food. The chefs work hard to create a menu filled with something that will satisfy each and every palate. While many a Sheffield public house is struggling to survive, The Peacock seems to go from strength to strength with a good landlord, Simon, and with excellent bar staff and chefs – long may it thrive! One of the authors of this book, Michael Liversidge, is a very regular visitor at The Peacock, his favourite local. A quick tip food-wise, if you do go to The Peacock, is try the Sheffield Fishcake. You will not be disappointed! The Peacock also has a very distinctive and wonderfully ornate, hand-crafted wrought-iron pub sign.

Bibliography

Banks, W. A., *A Pub on Every Corner – A Directory of Local Hotels, Inns and Taverns.* (Self-published typeset manuscript. Undated).

Bellamy, E., Clammer, R. and Jones, J., *High Green in Times Past.* (A Countryside Publication, 1984).

F.A.B.C.O Local History Group, *Around the Nab* (Sheffield: Wildtrack Publishing, 2006).

Gillott, S., *Handsworth* (Stroud: Tempus Publishing, 1999).

Greaves, B., *Life and Times at Bracken Hill* (Sheffield: Chapeltown & High Green Archive, 1992).

Handley, C., Stapleton, B. and A. Rowles (eds), *Shire Brook: The Forgotten Valley* (Sheffield: ADL Design & Print, 2007).

Handley, C., and I. D. Rotherham, *Moor Memories of the Peak District* (Sheffield: Wildtrack Publishing, 2011).

Heeley History Workshop, *Heghlegh Then and Heeley Now* (Sheffield: Pickards Colour Publishing, 1988).

Jones, M. and J. Jones, *Ecclesfield, Chapeltown and High Green Through Time* (Stroud: Amberley, 2009).

Lamb, D., *A Pub on Every Corner* (Sheffield: The Hallamshire Press, 1996).

Liversidge, M., *The Definitive A to Z Listing of Sheffield Public Houses* (Sheffield: Pickards Colour Publishing, 1999).

Morley, C., *Grenoside: A Brief Historical Survey* (Sheffield: PAM Print, 1996).

Salim, V., *A Ghost Hunter's Guide to Sheffield* (Sheffield: Sheaf Publishing, 1983).

Salim, V., *More Sheffield Ghosts and Where to Find Them* (Sheffield: Sheaf Publishing, 1987).

Tuffrey, P., *Sheffield Pubs: Landlords and Landladies* (Stroud: Fonthill Media, 2012).

Vickers, E. J., *Old Sheffield Town – An Historical Miscellany* (Sheffield: Applebaum Bookshop Limited, 1978).

Wasteneys, H., *Grenoside Recollections* (Sheffield: University of Sheffield Printing Unit, 1980).

Widdowson, L. and M. Young, *Woodhouse* (Stroud: Chalford Publishing Co., 1996).

About the Authors

Ian D. Rotherham is professor of Environmental Geography and reader in Tourism and Environmental Change at Sheffield Hallam University. An ecologist and environmental historian, he is a worldwide authority on landscape history and urban environments. He has been researching and writing about Sheffield for many years and has campaigned for its conservation, improvement and its wider promotion. He has published over 400 papers, articles, books and book chapters, has a popular BBC Radio Sheffield phone-in, and writes for local and regional newspapers, particularly the *Sheffield Star* and the *Yorkshire Post*. Ian is a regional tourism ambassador for Sheffield and South Yorkshire, and was formerly the principal city ecologist and director of ecological services for Sheffield. He was actively involved in the regeneration of the Industrial Lower Don Valley in the 1980s and 1990s, and led work to develop a series of over twelve major nature reserves in and around the city. He is honorary chair of the Sheffield Partnership for Rivers in the Town Environments. He has written widely about Sheffield and the wider region and his local books include *Lost Sheffield in Colour*, *Lost Nottingham in Colour*, *Sherwood and the Dukeries*, *Lost York in Colour*, and *Secret Sheffield* (with Melvyn Jones and Christine Handley). His knowledge of the pubs and clubs of Sheffield goes back to the 1970s and 1980s, first as a local resident and then as a student.

Michael Liversidge is a director of two printing companies and co-editor of a local Sheffield-based magazine. Upon leaving school in 1963, he was employed as an apprentice compositor and has worked within the printing industry continuously for the last fifty-three years.

He has produced eight local interest books on such diverse subjects including: *Attercliffe*, two books about the area of Sheffield he was born and raised in; *Time Gentlemen Please*; *Sheffield Wednesday; Sheffield United; Postcards from Sheffield* and recently collaborated with C. Eyre a local historian *on Football in Sheffield*. In addition to this, Michael is a regular contributor to the local newspaper, the *Sheffield Star*, and to other local magazines.

Married to Ann for nearly half a century, Michael has two children, Mark and Clair, and three grandchildren, Daniel, Abigail and Amy.

He could, at one stage in the 1980s, point to the fact that he's had a drink in every public house in Sheffield. With all the new drinking establishments opening over the last few years, and Michael's drinking curtailed through health issues, this is something he can, sadly, no longer boast about.

Christine Handley has an MA in History and a Certificate in Local History. She was born and brought up in Sheffield and developed an early interest in exploring hidden corners of Sheffield through weekly family trips to the local countryside. Her particular interests are in industrial and landscape history, using maps and other documentary evidence to investigate the evolution of places and in discovering the unusual and distinctive in buildings and monuments. She has worked on a variety of community-based projects dealing with both the built and natural environments passing on her enthusiasm and experience to get people to uncover the past that is all around them. This extends to looking at local pubs and their place in the local community. With Ian Rotherham and Melvyn Jones, she co-authored *Secret Sheffield* for Amberley Publishing. She has co-written and edited a number of other volumes with Ian Rotherham.